Cosimo Melani: The Chianti Countryside

Cover photo:
Cloisters of the ancient fortified country church of the Castle in San Polo in Rosso (Gaiole in Chianti)

JOURNEY TO THE CHIANTI

GETTING TO KNOW AN ANCIENT TUSCAN REGION

TO THE INHABITANTS OF THE CHIANTI

This is an account of a journey between past and present.
A journey that began many years ago and is still going on.

florence packaging

"The Tuscan countryside was planned like the work of art of a refined population, the same population that commissioned its artists to create paintings and frescos in the Quattrocento: this is the principle distinguishing feature to be found in the pattern of the fields, the architecture of Tuscan buildings. These people built their rural landscapes as if they were only concerned with beauty. The Tuscan countryside is arranged like a garden. In a way, the painters of their cities also contributed towards idealizing their countryside, especially the low hillsides near the urban centres."

Henri Desplannques

LEONARDO CASTELLUCCI

JOURNEY TO THE CHIANTI

GETTING TO KNOW AN ANCIENT TUSCAN REGION

photography: Gian Luigi Scarfiotti

Louis Gauffierre: *Portrait of Dr. Penrose, 1799*
Minneapolis, Institute of Arts

florence packaging

ACKNOWLEDGMENTS:

TOWN COUNCILS OF THE CHIANTI

LAURA BIANCHI, CASTELLO DI MONSANTO, FOR THE PHOTO ON P. 135
BANCA DEL CHIANTI FIORENTINO (SAN CASCIANO VAL DI PESA) FOR THE PHOTOS ON PP. 59, 60 ,61
CONSORZIO MARCHIO STORICO, FONDAZIONE LEGA DEL CHIANTI E TERRE DEL CHIANTI FOR THE PHOTOS ON P. 58
AGRICOLA QUERCIABELLA FOR THE PHOTO ON P. 181
DIEVOLE S.P.A FOR THE PHOTOS ON PP. 183, 184, 185
AZIENDA AGRICOLA SAN FELICE FOR THE PHOTOS ON PP. 176,177
CASTELLO DI GABBIANO FOR THE PHOTOS ON PP. 148,149

THE ARCHAEOLOGISTS ENRICO CIABATTI AND GIULIA PETTENA
ARCHITECT SPARTACO MORI
RAFFAELLO BARBARESI

WE WISH TO THANK:

THE MELANI FAMILY FOR THE WORK BY MILO MELANI PUBLISHED ON P. 165
THE DEL POGGETTO FAMILY FOR THE WORK BY MILO MELANI PUBLISHED ON P. 95
VENTURINO VENTURI FOR HAVING GIVEN PERMISSION TO PUBLISH HIS WORK ON P. 179

OUR SPECIAL THANKS TO
GIOVANNI BRACHETTI MONTORSELLI

CONCEIVED AND EDITED BY FLORENCE PACKAGING – FLORENCE

EDITED BY LEONARDO CASTELLUCCI AND MONICA MANESCALCHI

TEXT: LEONARDO CASTELLUCCI

PHOTOGRAPHY: GIAN LUIGI SCARFIOTTI

TRANSLATION: ALICE SCOTT

TRANSLATION: LAURA MARKELL: PP. 44, 45/82-85/146-149/156-159/176,177/182-185

WATERCOLOUR: COSIMO MELANI

GRAPHIC DESIGN: COSIMO MELANI

STYLING: COSIMO MELANI, FILIPPO GINI

EDITING: THOMAS BOURKE - LAURA MARKELL

PHOTOLITHOGRAPHY: SUONI E ARMONIE S.R.L. FIESOLE (FLORENCE) ITALY

PHOTOGRAPHS by

ROBERTO QUAGLI FOR THE PHOTOS ON PP. 44, 45
GIOVANNI CORTI FOR THE PHOTOS ON PP. 82, 84, 146, 147, 156-159

ISBN 88-901079-3-6

PUBLISHED BY FLORENCE PACKAGING AND ARTE TIPOLITOGRAFICA ITALIANA SPA
© FLORENCE PACKAGING, IDEE PER L'EDITORIA
VIA COSIMO IL VECCHIO 5, FLORENCE - ITALY
E-MAIL: florence.packaging@libero.it
E-MAIL: monmanes@tin.it
www.florencepackaging.books.com

ON THE COVER:
Cloisters of the ancient fortified country church of the castle in San Polo in Rosso

CONTENTS

AGER CLANTIVS
ET EIVS OPPIDA

A STRIP OF LAND
BETWEEN TWO ANCIENT CITIES

he adjectives that easily become rhetorical – for it should be remembered that there was a very sophisticated art of rhetoric of ancient origin which is no longer taught today – are the first that emerge in the minds of those who want to write about this region, but it is a temptation one should try to avoid. Well then, let us face the difficult task of communicating personal suggestions and impressions through the written word, trying not to fall into the shallow trivialities of certain pompous and general descriptions.

Travelling to the Chianti implies visiting a well kept countryside, where spontaneous nature is dominated by low oak woods, where there are also black hornbeams and chestnut trees, rows of poplars and isolated alders, along the protected areas that have a long existence near water sources. Among the spontaneous thickets are visible junipers and the bright yellow tufts of sweet-smelling broom, a natural flora that grows amidst vast spaces in which to move and expand. But these spaces are shared with vineyards and olive trees that cover entire slopes, giving us an impression of their being scanty and less invasive. Indeed, olive trees are small, cultivated, spiritual trees both pleasant and soothing to look at. Just try to take a walk in a large olive grove and in the repetitive and slightly nerve-wracking, however beautiful, maze of a vineyard . In the land of olive trees, one seems to belong to a world which recalls the slow, interior rhythms of meditation, leaving sufficient space and light. Instead, in the land of vines, you are in the centre of a feast, crowded with shrubs, foliage and large bunches of ripe grapes that capture your attention, grip and inebriate you.

One impression, shared also by others, is that there are no longer peasants in the Chianti. Maybe you do not see them because of the rough territory, interrupted by valleys and hillsides. You may catch a glimpse of someone driving a tractor in the distance, but these are only fleeting impressions - tiny men swallowed by an overflowing countryside. However they do exist, moving slowly in large crowds towards the vineyards and working solidly during the harvesting when the grapes of Sangiovese are ready to change their name and harvesting Chianti. They are always present - old men, sons, grand-children, relatives and so many young people coming from the urban centres and cities to give a hand, learning to do something useful. And above all they come to take part in a joyful ritual which goes back to the origins of the world. This ritual is repeated again two months later when the very same people who took part in the grape harvesting also assist in the olive picking. They stretch a large sheet around each tree and climb to pick the olives which are then harvested and pressed to obtain the healthiest, most tasty and gleaming of all natural fats.

The origins of

a name... to drink

Some people claim that the name Chianti probably derives from that of an important ancient Etruscan family.

Others think that the word comes from the Latin word clango *which means to sound the trumpets.*

We all have our own ideas about the countryside. Some dream of thick woodlands, with streams flowing through where animals stop to quench their thirst and, at the slightest rustle, rush to take shelter in the thick vegetation; others see it as being more airy and open, with large fields stretching as far as the hill sides that merge with the horizon; those who want to avoid the extremes of an undulating, peaceful and well ordered landscape might prefer to get closer to the Chianti near Siena where you can catch glimpses of severe, bare hills or fragments of a 'minimalist' countryside, devoid of almost all vegetation which then become slopes embellished by the charming elegance of an isolated farmhouse and irregular rows of cypresses. But there are some who also associate the idea of the countryside with an entirely human concept. In this case it is covered with vineyards, olive groves, vegetable gardens and enclosed with stone walls and pebbled country lanes which announce the existence of neighbouring human life in farms and villages. The parish priests are there to open the ancient doors of the numerous Romanesque churches. With their slim and friendly figures they transmit the idea of a more human God. Hence, in the Chianti everyone can find a place for his own peace of mind as this area has the enormous gift of changing, thanks to a versatility and creativity intolerant of all forms of boredom.

In the words of the great French historian Fernand Braudel, the Chianti is the "most inspiring countryside that exists".

Therefore, seduced by such uplifting poetry, we start off with the idea of travelling to a place which is excessively praised and which can, perhaps... move us in some way.

A land between two ancient cities
Let us imagine a Chianti devoid of vineyards and olive groves, without its castles, churches, farmhouses and even without its people. We have to stretch our imagination to visualize this area four thousand years ago without its age-old reference points. Long before the arrival of the Etruscans, there lived in these areas men clad in animal skins using rudimental stone and bronze weapons and living on hunting. They were small, semi-nomad tribes scattered between the centre and north of the peninsula. Archaeologists have united these people under the appealing and mysterious term 'Civilization of the Rinaldone Culture', just as they do in art history with paintings stylistically attributable to an individual painter but whose identity cannot be traced.

Let us leave these early ancestors of remote times behind us and return to a more clearly documented era, back to the Etruscans who have left more consistent signs of their long, stable presence in the Chianti. Important findings exist in the archaeological collection of Castellina in Chianti where there are small necropoli that one can visit and people who show a great interest in archaeology. Moreover, the Etrusco-Latin etymology which identifies the names of places in the Chianti reveals bited for at least 2500 years. After the Etruscans, there were the Romans who brought with them a flourishing society building a rich, 'modern' road network. This period was followed by long centuries of abandonment and oblivion. In feudal times, the slow but regular increase of the population and the recovery of trade, also stimulated by the proximity of the road which went from Rome to the other side of the Alps, via Francigena, brought new wealth to the territory. It had long been the scenario of fierce contentions between Arezzo and Siena and, soon after, between Siena and an increasingly arrogant Florence which had expanded its territories more and more throughout Tuscany from the 12th century on.

It was then that the Chianti changed its appearance, gradually absorbing the architectural connotations which were to distinguish it in the following centuries as it became the centre of disputes between these two proud rivals until the definitive annexation of Siena under the jurisdiction of the Medici. The Chianti was a battlefield and the people of the contado lived a truly insecure period which did not favour the growth of agriculture. Only after the conclusion of this old contention, did this area resume a systematic development in its agriculture and wine growing.

Vasari paints the Chianti

In the Palazzo Vecchio can be seen the grandiose representation of the figure of triumph and glory. Both celebrate and praise Cosimo I of the Medici who with the strength of arms and strategy defeated all his rivals, placing himself at the height of a power destined to last in time. The fame of these numerous victories was to leave its mark on history. Cosimo commissioned Giorgio Vasari, his court painter – no doubt a more valid architect and art historian – to illustrate the victories of the Florentine troops on the walls and ceiling of the sumptuous Sala dei Cinquecento in the Palazzo Vecchio or, if you prefer, Palazzo della Signoria. And, amidst the clangour of arms and the stampede of horses, of faces tried by exertion, pain and terror, is visible a painting with a fine structural approach, the 'Allegory of Clante' where all the subjects and symbols that identify this region are illustrated. It is clearly inspired by the cartoons of the Battles of Anghiari and Cascina, abandoned years before by Leonardo and Michelangelo somewhere in the Palazzo. In the foreground, emerges the figure of an old pensive Bacchus which is the foreshorned centre of the composition.

Just behind, an armed youth holds a large shield on which is depicted the symbol of the ancient League: from two priceless vases, gush the waters of the rivers Elsa and Pesa, which flow through the territory and, below, illuminated by a glowing light recalling the flames of a battle, are the strongholds of Castellina, Radda and Brolio, the noble fortifications representing the Florentine supremacy.

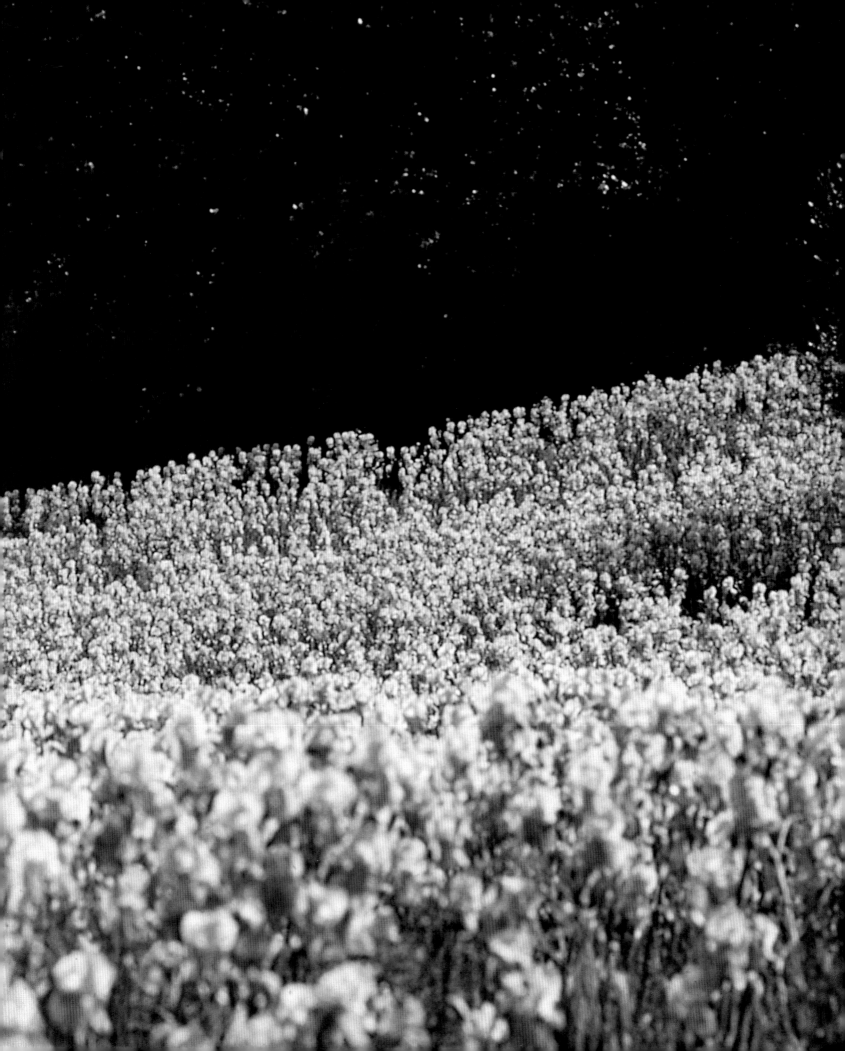

THIS, MY LORD, IS THE CHIANTI, WITH THE PESA RIVER AND THE ELSA, WITH HORNS FULL OF FRUIT, AT THE FOOT OF WHICH IS A MATURE BACHUS, FOR THE EXCELLENT WINES OF THAT TERRITORY; IN THE DISTANCE I HAVE PAINTED CASTELLINA, RADDA AND BROLIO, WITH THEIR EMBLEMS; AND THE WEAPON ON THE SHIELD HELD BY THAT YOUTH WHO REPRESENTS THE CHIANTI, IS A BLACK COCK IN A YELLOW FIELD.

GIORGIO VASARI

LIVING IN STONE

DWELLINGS OF THE CHURCH
THE SIGNORI AND THE CONTADO

DWELLINGS OF THE CHURCH
THE SIGNORI AND THE CONTADO

The stone of the Chianti, that stone with which castles, farmhouses, churches and important abbeys were built for a long period in the Middle Ages, is Alberese, a sandstone which is not the only stone used but one which distinguishes the building heritage of this territory.

Alberese is a rock, containing a large amount of calcite that can be easily recognized by a very fine, friable grain and a whitish colour, often heightened by dark streaks varying in tone that range from ivory white to iron grey. The medieval building fabric was constructed with this stone. Hence, the pointed and rounded arches of the early Romanesque churches, the resistant fortresses, attenuated by the light tones of Alberese, the same light tones found on the farmhouses.

Later, new ideas came from Florence. Early signs of the Renaissance began to appear on the palaces of the Signori which were often sumptuous country villas covered with plaster, with windows and doors framed with pietra serena. On the one hand, these solutions added more colour to the landscape, but on the other, there was something superfluous coming from the city to a territory which had been identified only by solid stone walls. The new Florentine architecture gradually imposed itself even if numerous contemporary buildings preserved their rustic stone façades.

**Church of
San Donato in Poggio**

Churches in pure Romanesque style

Romanesque churches, lsiòilar to, yet more so than the beautiful farmhouses and medieval fortresses, are a constant reference point throughout the Chianti. Although they vary in size and often in shape, these buildings serve as precious documents of Romanesque architecture in Tuscany. Abbeys, churches and suffragan chapels testify to the existence of a populated and organized region. Moreover, the ancient road to France which connected Rome to the other countries beyond the Alps, brought pilgrims, wayfarers, merchants and wealth. But it also introduced new ideas. This is probably why there exist not only numerous, very simple Tuscan Romanesque churches but also a few significant examples of buildings in the Romanesque style coming from Lombardy and Ravenna. Proof of this is given by the churches of San Pietro in Bossolo near Tavarnelle and Sant'Appiano in the vicinity of Barberino Val d'Elsa, both originally conceived with "an octagonal baptistry with walls internally marked by blind arches in a tradition to be found in the baptistries of Ravenna".

Typical of our Romanesque style is the church of San Donato in Poggio, which stands in an isolated position just outside the village with the same name. Inside, the nave and two aisles are divided by simple, quadrilateral columns without other decorations and the roof is in solid wood, following the taste of the Chianti Romanesque style. This sober architecture often led "to the suppression of the external arches above the apses".

Castles

Castles are to be found everywhere, but this is not the Loire valley! Nor are there impossible rocks above which those towers rise like the pointed lances that distinguish German castles in fairy tales or the epic Anglo-Saxon manor-houses which take us back to the innocence of our childhood and which can, at an 'unsuitable' age, evoke the memories of noble dames on horseback, locked up for love in impenetrable castles.

The castles of the Chianti have a human dimension and although medieval fortresses were built for reasons of war, they now appear less challenging as they have taken on the appearance of fortified noble villas with those mixed, architecturally varied characteristics, capable of blending the sturdiness of an embattled tower with a peaceful plastered façade added two centuries later, or a cloistered barrel vaulted cellar with a romantic garden. They are 'penitent' fortifications which have, with time, laid down their arms to espouse the noble cause of peace.

Although they have departed from their original plan, most of these castles in the Chianti still preserve those architectural elements, typical of these imposing defensive structures. Italo Moretti describes them perfectly: "The architectural structure is typical of the Middle Ages: their development along a road of access, or opening like a fan on the slope of a hill with the main elements on the top (keep, palace, church) or in concentric circles, following the contours of the hill. On the lowlands the architectural structure is often more regular".

Castle of Meleto

Green gardens

There is also a Chianti of gardens, a Chianti that hides varying extensions behind the walls of its castles, villas and abbeys where they can apply an art which has always been popular in Italy, namely landscape gardening, Italian gardens or romantic parks. In Italian gardens, rational thinking dominates nature giving it a shape and exact geometric patterns, at times they are also full of complex arrangements. Low box hedges outline labyrinthine geometric forms in the search for aesthetic gratification but maybe also in a desire for the mysterious. Then there are romantic parks which forget the 'cold, orderly' geometric forms in favour of a spontaneous nature, if only on the surface, reproduced to scale inside a private garden.

Garden of the
Badia a Coltibuono

THE JOURNEY

In the beginning there were the Etruscans

An eye trained to look at architectural forms has no difficulty in identifying the typical building style of the Chianti. It all began in the Middle Ages and continued to develop in the following centuries. Yet these lands were inhabited by the Etruscans and life was also intense and stable in the long period of Roman civilization. However, very little has survived from that long span of time and maybe a great deal has still to be discovered.

Let us stop at Cetamura, probably together with Castellina, the most extensive centre of Etruscan Chianti civilization. It is an important site which also includes the nearby localities of Sestaccia and Campi. The gate of Cetamura is still standing. It seems to be the setting for a play that will never take place, a stone gate surrounded by the country-side. A stone gate is all that remains of the medie-val settlement and the castle. This is Cetamura today. However, recent excavations in which archaeologists from Florida University also took part, made it possible for us to write the history of the settlement, one of the oldest of all the Etruscan Chianti. In this settlement which survived until Roman times, a small quarter for craftsmen was brought to light, dating back to the 3rd-2nd cen-tury B.C. where there was a small furnace for baking bricks and tiles. This implied that clay was used as a building material in the Chianti long before the advent of Christ. Archaeological research is still active throughout this region which goes to prove that we are only at the beginning of this important return to the past. However, a lack of visible documentation stimulates the imagina-tion. This isolated but magnificent entrance to the countryside is sufficient for us to dedicate our attention to a people that no longer exists and to their daily life.

The Etruscans of Castellina

The district of Castellina in Chianti is the one where most of the archeological findings of the Etruscans have been unear-thed. There is not a real museum but many materials have been removed from the tombs of the area and exhibi-ted in the atrium of the medie-val castle. Among the most important objects are also two attic amphoras and 'black figu-res', attributable to the 6th cen-tury BC, which come from the necropolis of the nearby centre of Fonterutoli, as shown in the photo.

Coming across a Roman bridge

The road map leaves no doubts. Ponte agli Stolli is outside the sacred confines of the Chianti Classico and should therefore be excluded from our journey. But how can we give up the joy of breaking a rule only to go back and make it our own? What I mean is, to break a rule for more lofty ends. Well then, if we go beyond the boundaries for a few hundred metres to reach this destination, we do not feel we are offending anybody. On the contrary, we are doing them a favour by giving information and, above all, contributing to the pleasure of discovery. Hidden by a thick row of trees and shrubs a small and gushing waterfall flows into a lake. Above it is a little bridge which is not particularly striking but is almost two thousand years old, a Roman bridge renamed Ponte agli Stolli. It is one of the numerous testimonies of the vast road network of the Roman Chianti.

From a noteworthy study published by the Centro di Studi Chiantigiani "Clante", we are informed that a large Roman road of late imperial times passed through these areas, that is, in the Valdarno Superiore - the upper Arno valley. The road was commissioned by Emperor Hadrian, remembered in history as a tolerant ruler, capable of re-establishing an empire which revealed the first evident signs of decline. This very able leader adopted the new, modern road to replace the old, dilapidated consular one, the Cassia, already recorded at the time as irreparably lost, *vetustate collapsum,* that is closed to traffic due to excessive wear and tear. He did this to improve the links between Rome and Florence which had become the richest and most powerful city of Tuscia.

The road of the Florentine castles

The road of the Chiantigiana which connects Strada in Chianti to Greve is an open stretch of countryside, a part of the Florentine Chianti where the lowland blends with gentle harshness. In this short stretch, are situated some of the most important ancient fortresses of the entire territory. The castle of Vicchiomaggio which probably originally belonged to a Longobard noble family until the 12th century, was surrounded by a large circle of battlements but, like many other similar structures, has undergone destruction and reconstruction in the course of the centuries. Indeed, in some parts it reminds us of an authentic medieval castle, while in other parts, neo-Gothic features can be observed. Some very fine Chianti Classico wines are produced in this area and there exists a specific form of agricultural tourism for those in search of the atmosphere of castles. A hundred metres further on, another gigantic stone building draws the visitor's attention. To reach the entrance, it is necessary to cross a dirt road. All around, vast 'vineyards' show the wine producing vocation of the castle. It is the castle of Verrazzano, dating back to the 10th-11th centuries, situated in a place where there had been an Etruscan settlement many years before. In 1485, the famous explorer and navigator Giovanni da Verrazzano who discovered the Hudson bay, was born here. In this case too, only a few ruins of the old

At the 'Court of the Princes'

Villa le Corti is one of the most imposing villas of the Chianti. You can get there through an ancient avenue of cypresses. The lovely Renaissance windows on the first floor seem to depart from the regal doorway surmounted by an arch from which protrudes a large coat of arms of the family of the Corsini princes who have been the owners of this 13th century building since 1427. In the course of time it has taken on the form of a sturdy fortified villa where you can spend the night in three fine apartments tasting the excellent wines produced on the estate.

The castle of Pier Soderini

The most outstanding features of the Castle of Gabbiano are the circular towers. This building was also the property of Pier Soderini who as a Gonfalonier, ruled Florence from 1502. Subsequently, it looked more like a rural villa but preserved its fortified aspect. Here we had the pleasure of tasting what seemed to us the pièce par excellence of the selected production of Azienda Aria, a Supertuscan wine, a pure Sangiovese which gives elegant musty aromas.

fortress have survived, considering that the most important part of the architectural complex is reminiscent of the forms of a noble Florentine villa begun in 1600 and concluded in later periods. Here too, excellent wines are produced which are accompanied by a refined hospitality.

If we proceed towards Greve, it is a must to stop in one of the most fascinating buildings of the Chianti, Villa Calcinaia, a fine example of 16th century building in the Florentine countryside. The villa has a long, low façade with a sober plan and simple lines. In front of the entrance is a beautiful Italian garden. The earls Capponi, owners of the building since 1524, transformed the pre-existing building into the present one, creating its present day activity. This activity has always been based on wine production which has been recently improved thanks to an accurate selection of the grapes. The Riserva Villa Calcinaia is a wine for highly sophisticated palates. Before entering Greve, a road sign leads us to the Castle of Uzzano. A solid ring of walls reminding us of the original fortified complex surrounds an elegant 15th century villa with its façade marked by the columns of a noble loggia. The vast Italian garden extending from the rear façade is noteworthy. A few small ancient buildings used for tourist facilities face a charming courtyard.

Benedictine echoes

When it appears in the distance, it looks like a castle. There is nothing to make you suspect that inside those imposing, unfriendly walls, there exists an intense religious life. The Benedictine monks built it in 890 on the ruins of a Longobard fortress. In such spiritually restless times which had given rise to the great monastic reforms of St. Benedict in the western world, in opposition to the decline of the power of the Roman Church, many saintly men had honestly tried to return to the essence of the message of Christ. Among them was also St. Giovanni Gualberto who gave life to the so-called reform of Vallombrosa, sustained by the monks of Badia a Passignano where the saint spent the last days of his life and died in 1073. For many years the abbey became an important spiritual centre of the Florentine countryside. The building we want to visit today, known as San Michele, is the result of several transformations which took place between the 13th and 15th centuries and of vast late 19th century neogothic style reconstruction. If we exclude the grandiose structures which form the abbey complex, we have to concentrate our attention mainly on the

San Biagio, saved from looting and heavy restoration, it has preserved its original plan of a Romanesque basilica with a precious crypt with cross vaults.

We must not enter the church before having carefully examined the façade showing the essential purity of the 13th century stylistic features. Inside, there is a rich collection of Renaissance paintings relating episodes of the life of the patron saint or founding father. We can admire the works of artists such as Michele di Ridolfo del Ghirlandaio, one of the most eclectic representatives of the early Tuscan Style and then go on to masters like Il Passignano, Giovanni Maria Butteri and Alessandro Vignamaggio.

GHIRLANDAIO'S LAST SUPPER

In the refectory of Badia a Passignano, we can see the large fresco, painted between 1476 and 1477 by Domenico Ghirlandaio, not yet thirty years old. After this first test on such a delicate theme, he was commissioned to paint the same subject also in other important Florentine churches and the contado. First, the church of Ognissanti. The style of Ghirlandaio was still influenced by a certain academic immobility which does not reach the excellent results of his mature works but it is clearly visible in the expressive faces of the Apostles sitting next to Jesus Christ, already conceived as natural portraits. His non-rhetorical and undramatic style is a typical feature as is the limitation of this important figure of the Florentine Renaissance, sometimes unjustly underestimated by artistic historiography.

HOUSES OF THE CHIANTI

The Farmhouse

If we refer to commonly used scientific terms, we may come round to the idea that Tuscans have a sense of order and moderation written in their genes. That sensitive eye for proportion expressed in the need of transforming every single article, fruit of their manual ability and imagination into something beautiful (besides, this is obvious from the fact that the Baroque has never taken root in these parts). It was a gift, or more simply, one aspect of their natural way of being, even in the case of peasants who were only familiar with the art of cultivating the land. This is still more

evident in the building of houses. These people who never moved from their homes throughout their lives and never gained external knowledge about what was beautiful, do not seem to have had to exert themselves to combine the need of a functional and practical dwelling where the kitchen became the symbolic place in the centre of the surrounding rooms with their rustic but reliable instinct for proportions and the sobriety of their forms. They were not only the poor, solid houses of simple, practical people, but humble dwellings in remarkably good taste.

The Chianti Farmhouse

"Contrary to what is generally believed, the farm-houses were not initially inhabited by peasants. They were the dwellings of the lower ranks of the nobility or of small proprietors. Frequently, the farmhouse was built on the ruins of the old abandoned castle, the tower became the dovecot in the centre of the living quarters. It was only in the Renaissance and with the improvement of living conditions both for the owners and the peasants, that the farmhouse took on its present aspect as the home of sharecropper, while the well-to-do who go there to spend their holidays, convert them into villas".

"The typical farmhouse in the form of a cube or para-llelepiped is distinguished by a spacious loggia (beginning of 12th century), by one, two or more large porches, which provide a large covered space, where it was possible to work exploiting the sunlight till dusk (...) The dovecot tower, characteristic of buildings in the Valdarno and the Chianti contribute to making them look lighter. It is usually surmounted by a single or double window and wider porches sometimes set in the centre of the main body of the building, or on one side. At others still, it is placed at the two ends of the farmhouse paired with another".

Enrico Bosi

A Baptistry of the imagination

There is nothing sumptuous or unusually spiritual about it. However it stirs the emotions and a somewhat mysterious atmosphere pervades. The romantic church of Sant'Appiano built on the former ruins of a Roman structure does not capture our attention through seduction, even if most of the interior with a nave and two aisles divided by rustic cotto columns still reveals elements that are mainly original. Nevertheless the most appealing feature is the erect and isolated columns in front of the façade which have grown pink and scaly with time. It is all that remains of the 7th to 8th century BC showing the Romanesque influence of Ravenna.

Two mullioned windows by a renowned artist

Dedicated to one of the finest preachers of the Florentine countryside, the church of San Cresci is a small Romanesque jewel. In spite of several unsuccessful changes, two delightful mullioned windows have been preserved on the narthex, the colours of which stand out against the white alberese stone and the red cotto.

The house of Monna Lisa

"Look, I am a countryman, and can you imagine in what corner of the earth, under what sky, I feel truly in a state of bliss? This place is called Vignamaggio from the vines of Bacchus and the month of the year when nature is in full bloom. It is surrounded on all sides by magnificent vineyards and this lovely spot in spring deserved this name". So wrote Valerio Chimentelli in a letter addressed to Alessandro Strozzi. This definition of being a countryman reveals a sense of pride and a privileged status expressed in a state of bliss. What Chimentelli wants to say is that the height of this sensation, reserved only to those who can enjoy the favours of nature and the countryside can be reached in this very spot, in Vignamaggio, in this stately villa where slightly less than two centuries before, probably in 1497, a baby girl destined by the stars to become the most notorious and admired feminine face of all times, Monna Lisa or *'La Gioconda'* came into the world. This mystic figure seems to have lived her earthly life between Florence and her birthplace in the Chianti, without any real tragedies, until her death in 1533, certainly not realizing how much the portrait she had commissioned from the young Master Leonardo was destined to appeal to the popular imagination of future centuries. Who knows if those enigmatic eyes and that mysterious smile really belonged to her?

The villa, now considered one of the finest examples of the Florentine Renaissance in the Chianti, shows the best of itself on the rear façade, in a dark pink plaster, typical of the Tuscan countryside. This rear façade looks onto an enchanting large park, planned and realized with enthusiasm by the former owner, the writer Bino Sanminiatelli, in ancient Italian landscape gardening traditions.

A lighthouse on a green sea

The keep of the Castle of Grignano and the few structures around it are all that remain of the ancient castle with the same name already existing in the 11th century. There are many other examples of similar transformations in the area, fortified structures that have only preserved a few parts of the original building in the course of time.

Pure Lombard Romanesque

On the road that leads to Borgo di Volpaia, we find the church of Santa Maria Novella that once held its jurisdiction over a vast territory. Unfortunately, its beauty has been ruined by unaesthetic 19th century restorations which have covered a great deal of the original Romanesque structure. The interior, divided into a nave and two aisles by columns and pillars, reveals, still intact, the Romanesque capitals with animal motifs that testify to their Lombard Romanesque origin.

MONTEFIENALI,
THE RETURN FROM OBLIVION

There is a part of the Chianti yet to be discovered. A Chianti beautiful for its nature and architecture. A Chianti where the vines have been replaced with fir and chestnut trees, and where the olive groves appear less frequently. Where the animal life prevails over that of man. It is a mountainous part of the Chianti countryside that lies on the border with the Apennine mountains. In fact it is where Valdarno begins. I slipped into the wood on the lookout for medieval village of Montefienali.

My curiosity had been roused on reading a volume that spoke of its restoration and its architectural value. I am a witness of its unique and beautiful history.

At the beginning of 1990 Montefienali, that stands on the western slope of the Apennine range of the Monti del Chianti, at 600 metres on the western slopes of Monte Luco, was a relict amongst the vegetation, a block of stone that was abandoned and lost over time. Then it was noticed and in those last, disconnected stones, someone managed to see what others had failed to notice.

Someone managed to image the ruins restored to their ancient origins, and the beauty and architectural value of the precarious building was envisaged. At the time it seemed a hazardous bet to place and perhaps it was, but today, that village, that reminds us of a noble Florentine estate, the Albizzi estate, is reliving its history, at least the aesthetical part, by showing off its original architectural credentials after restoration and reconstruction work that has entirely changed the cause of an attentive, meticulous and reconstructive philology that is the additional value of work which took three years to complete.

On the sides of the building there are the old houses of the village. A little lower down we can see a small Romanesque chapel, named after San Domenico, with a web bell-tower that is incredibly well-preserved. And whilst the building has become a relay of measured elegance, the old houses have been bought by private individuals that have chosen to live in this exclusive and different atmosphere. It is a radical choice that can be made only by those who fall in love with the place.

As simple as a house

With a façade like a hut and those forms, reminiscent of a simple medieval building, the church of San Marcellino looks like a simple farmhouse. What we actually see is the successful result of a 19th century reconstruction, obtained with the use of building materials taken from the former building.

A stone toy

The Castle of Meleto has one captivating attraction. Other castles have an imposing, powerful shape. Brolio and Cacchiano for example emerge clear and large, giving the impression of binding and subjugating the hill. When you get there, you come up against a part with large corner towers which seems to be leaning against you but immediately afterwards, as if to apologize for this severe impact, it grows lighter ending in a small terrace-garden facing the vineyards and is there waiting for the first shot by the film troupe of a Visconti film which will never be made.

The Castle of Meleto is also captivating because, different from other more impressive structures, it has maintained an aesthetic coherence even if what we see today is the product of several modifications in the course of time. This castle takes us back to the times of Federico Barbarossa who gave it to the Firidolfi family, from then on known as the Firidolfi Meletesi.

The two corner towers, one of which still preserves its rare trussed top with brick arches, date back to a partial 15th century reconstruction while the central keep, which in this case seems to be embedded and protected between the towers, belongs to the original plan. This Florentine castle which was reconquered by the Sienese and then taken back by the Florentines, went towards a period of peace from the 16th century onwards, when going against its own nature, it gradually became a rich, family villa as is visible in the interior, decorated in 18th century taste with abundant stuccoes and frescos reminiscent of country life.

Brolio or 'dei Ricasoli Firidolfi'

The castle of Brolio is similar to the emblem of the Chianti, a sort of banner, the standard-bearer of an entire army of fortresses, many of which have forgotten their original characteristics. This is due to the fact that when you see it from far away, it looks powerful, solid, arrogant, redundant. You then discover that this is not how things really are. You discover that that circle of walls which is an irregular indestructible pentagon of stone, encloses within its boundaries a peaceful life brimming with activity. But these walls are the same as those existing at the end of the 15th century when the castle was destroyed by one of the numerous armed attacks made in those centuries, in this case by the Aragonese troops in favour of the Kingdom of Naples. These walls which trace the irregular pattern of a pentagon and are connected to five towers, develop on a perimeter of almost 500 metres all along the passageway. From this privileged position, can clearly be seen another red brick structure which is obviously inspired by the Sienese taste in building belonging to a period much closer to our times. After the entrance square, you have to raise your eyes to see the original castle-keep, the place where the owners of the castle, in ancient times, repeatedly locked themselves in an extreme defence against the enemy of the moment. Hence the 15th century walls, a castle-keep over two hundred years old and living quarters entirely rebuilt in the 19th century. The most recent part may be difficult to combine but a Sienese architect's efforts to blend the pre-existing structures is evident and so particular as to resemble a small castle built in a larger one. The small castle is actually a building with neo-Gothic forms with Guelph crenellated towers, two-mullioned and three-mullioned windows and all the list of building terms in that neo-medieval style that had come back into fashion almost two centuries ago. Today, the gates of this large castle are opened by the members of the Ricasoli Firidolfi family themselves who have lived there since 1141.The rooms are mainly a new 19th century version. Everywhere can be found banners, armour, tapestry, sail vaults and the stern faces of ancestors among whom that of Bettino Ricasoli, "the iron baron" who played such an active part in the creation of the Unity of Italy and who, as a brilliant oenologist, wrote the recipe of Chianti wine. Then there is the rich library, with a collection of books of inestimable value and also the archives of the history of this important family.

An 'armed' church

When you finally get there, after crossing the countryside from Lecchi to Radda in Chianti, it will be difficult for you to imagine that locked in this powerful fortified structure, built in different periods, partly a fortress and partly a country villa with a lovely covered loggia, is one of the most ancient churches in the Chianti. When consulting books to know more about it, you find that it is sometimes called a country church, in others a castle or even a villa. Actually, like other building complexes, the church-castle of Spaltenna, among those that have undergone the same experience, combines these three different aspects. It is like saying that it has a spiritual soul, the profane, stern aspect of an impregnable fortress and the warm, elegant atmosphere inside a rich, noble villa. If you continue to enquire, you will find that the church of San Polo already belonged to the Firidolfi Ricasoli family before 1000 and that in the 13th century, the Florentines had a solid wall built for its defence, which transformed a great deal of its early Romanesque structure. You also get to know that most of the main structure of the building is the result of a 15th century intervention aimed at giving the building that profane and warlike spirit we mentioned before and that the façade of the church was raised so high that it became part of the surroun-

One thousand years of wine

The magnificent ring of walls of Monteriggioni is now close to us. The territory of the Chianti Classico is about to enter the Val d'Elsa: The countryside in this last stretch of land has opened up and dropped. It has become a flat, open plain. A small road climbs towards a slope framed by woods. The woods cover Villa Cerna from sight. For over a century, this estate has belonged to the Cecchi family, producers of a famous make of wines. This fine, compact building we can see, is the result of extensions and transformations that took place ever since 1300. As the document in Latin says, in 1001, on this spot, there was a farm cultivated with vines: "tertia cum vinea super se habentes… et cum fundamentis et omnes edificiis earum una cum inferioribus et superioribus". *Meaning a thousand years of continuity for the wine and a hundred years for the Cecchi Family who include among other labels a Chianti Classico Riserva Villa Cerna as their prize wine, the highest achievement of an activity which has always been dedicated to wine.*

ding walls. The apse was turned into a semicircular tower and the slender bell-tower was widened to the point of taking on the appearance of a sturdy keep. However, when you enter the church, you realize that the Romanesque elements still exist. The nave and two aisles, divided by solid pillars, end in the beautiful Romanesque apse which has not lost its forms on the inside. Before leaving this composite building, your attention falls on a splendid cycle of 14th century frescos, attributed to the Sienese painters Cristoforo di Bindoccio and Meo di Pero. These frescos have survived all the changes and in the lunettes of the nave, they have told the *Stories of the Life of Christ* for seven centuries. The last work that draws our attention is the wooden Crucifix, also of the Sienese Trecento by an unknown artist. They are the only two important works of art that have remained from an even more significant collection in the church. Indeed those who wish to complete their 'visit' should go to the Pinacoteca of Siena to admire the fine Duecento painting by the Master of San Polo in Rosso, identified by many as Segni di Bonaventura. For many centuries, the *Crucifix* was a symbol of meditation and prayer for the inhabitants of this contado.

One should also admire some of the wines produced in 'limited quantities' by the firm with the same name. *The Castelpolo* and the *Chianti Classico reserves…* 'open the dance' for the wine-tasting.

THE CHIANTI IN THE MUSEUM
'SECLUDED' MASTERPIECES

Master of Montefioralle

Madonna and Child

Church of Santo Stefano

Montefioralle

Meliore di Jacopo

Madonna Enthroned

between Saint Peter and Saint Paul

Church of San Leolino

THE YOUNG AMBROGIO LORENZETTI

A short while ago, Baby Jesus was asleep, whereas now, his eyes are wide open for he can feel his mother pushing down her legs to get up and solemnly go towards her observer, to announce her divine regality. She still has the expression of an icon, fixed and lost in perfection. Contrarily, Jesus with surprised and credulous eyes suspended in a tangible, everyday situation, is the sign of a change, the sign of the modernity of the young master who in this painting of 1319, the first work attributed to him with certainty, already reveals the important elements of his style. It is true that the artist turns to Giotto and the Florentine school but as a Sienese, he does not forget the transparent colours of his fellow artists, Duccio and Simone Martini. This style becomes evident in a vigorous, expressive brushstroke and an almost reckless use of perspective, a problem presented by Giotto in Florence in a forced, 'illusionistic' key.

We are now standing in front of a *Madonna Enthroned* by Ambrogio Lorenzetti, belonging to the cycle of frescos entitled *The effects of Good and Bad Governance in Siena*. He is a father of the primitive school of painting, even if his complex, ingenious nature of a restless experimental artist makes us consider him as one beyond the rigid attribution of an artistic, historical category. The painting is now preserved in the Museum of Sacred Art of San Casciano, exposed in the church of Santa Maria del Gesù where you can appreciate a small but select collection of masterpieces coming from the area of San Casciano.

Near Lorenzetti's Madonna, there is a very

rare altar frontal, depicting *Saint Michael the Archangel and the Stories of the Legend* by the Florentine Coppo di Marcovaldo, who can be considered the first master and who, already in the first half of the 13th century, had felt the need to abandon the Byzantine, figurative stereotype. There is also a mysterious, impressive *Nativity,* probably a work by the Master of Cabestany. It is a marble torso, formerly in the church of San Giovanni in Sugana, full of a primitive charm, typical of Romanesque figures.

Coppo di Marcovaldo

Saint Michael the Archangel and

Stories of the Legend

Museum of Sacred Art

San Casciano in Val di Pesa

SIENESE INFLUENCE
AND FLORENTINE SUPREMACY

When examining the vast artistic heritage of the Chianti, we notice that most of the paintings collected in the small museums or still preserved in the religious buildings for which they were executed, date back to a period from the start of the 13th to the end of the 15th century, which has historical explanations. During these two centuries many paintings were commissioned for the numerous religious buildings which flourished in large numbers everywhere from the 12th century.

Indeed, in this period, the territory was repopulated, due to the encouragement of the city of Florence, which fortified the Chianti with hamlets and castles to exercise its control over Siena. Many churches requested an equal number of devotional works. However the works of the 13th and 14th century masters were distinguished by new ferments. Even if many of these artists are unknown, they are almost all of Florentine origin with their eyes turned towards Cimabue and especially to the influence of Giotto and consequently to that great innovative movement which sowed the seeds of the new painting, mainly in Florence, but also in Siena. Instead, the 15th century paintings are signed by serial masters who may excel in their technique and profession but show no interest in the revolutionary stirrings of the early Renaissance. This explains why the Chianti and many other areas of the Florentine countryside are teaming with delightful, elaborate works by Bicci di Lorenzo and his son, Lorenzo di Bicci whose forms are almost clones of his father's or his contemporary, Cenni di Francesco, all active in the first half of the Quattrocento and still painting in the international Gothic style, the affected swansong of a style of painting that had seen its century of glory in the 14th century. All this took place in spite of the fact that young Masaccio was painting the frescos of the Brancacci Chapel and Beato Angelico brought a different, more familiar idea of transcendency to his paintings and frescos.

Master of Cabestany

Nativity

Museum of sacred art

San Casciano in Val di Pesa

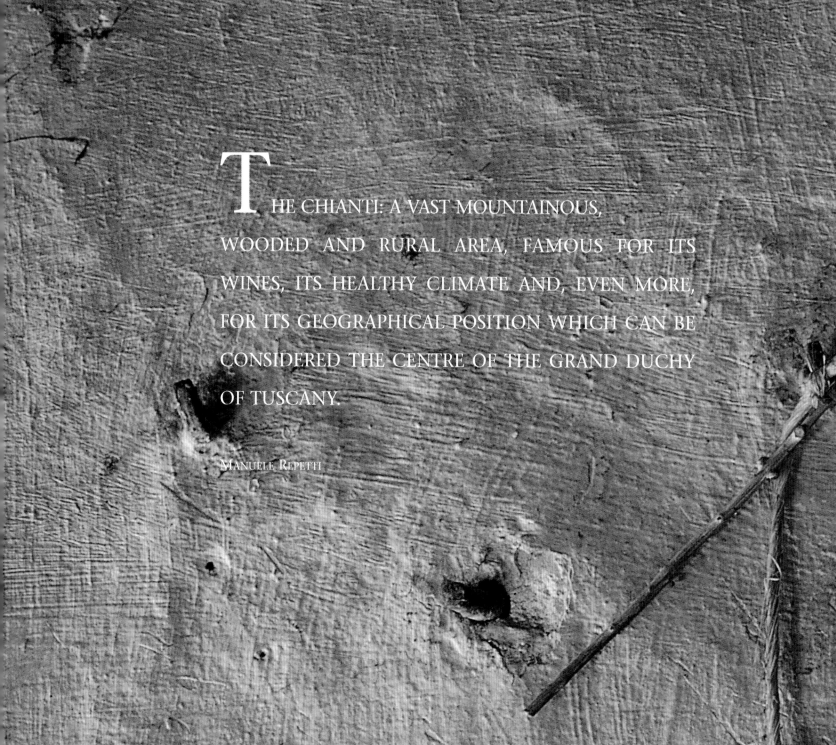

The Chianti: a vast mountainous, wooded and rural area, famous for its wines, its healthy climate and, even more, for its geographical position which can be considered the centre of the grand duchy of Tuscany.

Manuele Repetti

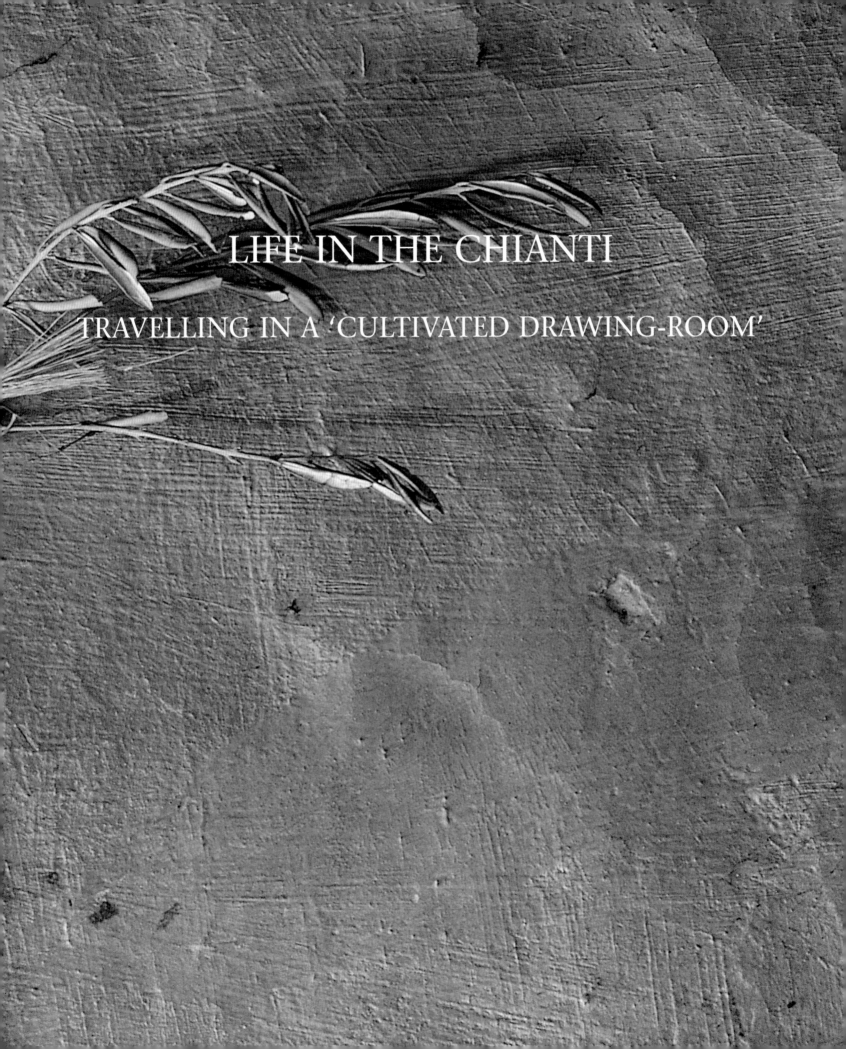

LIFE IN THE CHIANTI

TRAVELLING IN A 'CULTIVATED DRAWING-ROOM'

TRAVELLING IN A
'CULTIVATED DRAWING -ROOM'

In autumn, chestnuts are

gathered… on horseback

In some parts of the Chianti

covered with chestnut woods,

an ancient tradition has been

preserved. Specialists are invi-

ted to gather chestnuts for

which they are paid through

the nose. This should not

lead us to think that these

professionals come with the

latest and most sophisticated

machinery invented by the

most up-to-date technology.

They arrive on horseback just

like the butteri in Maremma

and, like acrobats, they reach

the highest branches of the

trees to gather their tasty

fruit.

t the beginning of the seventies, the Chianti was a territory that was still to be discovered. The land had been abandoned by the exodus of so many young people who had rushed to the cities a few years before, in search of more congenial and better paid work. This had also been the trend all over Italy. Then the English, Germans, Swiss, Americans, and lastly the more skilful and shrewd Italians put a stop to this unfortunate trend. They began to rehabilitate their buildings, mainly consisting of beautiful, stone farmhouses, large farms and numerous medieval fortresses which became again the homes of people speaking many languages with different ideas about life in general, and frequently also about making wine. Life resumed full growth, not in the sense of former times but a new life. There the Chianti became a sort of prototype of a new way of conceiving and understanding the countryside. A style of living that led to the coining of a new word abroad: "Chiantishire".

To someone like myself, born and brought up in Florence and still living here, torn between an innate pride of belonging and a less blissful state of cultural isolation, the term arouses a certain perplexity. The word, an exquisite, Anglo-Saxon invention, seems to have been coined by the American writer and journalist, Burton Anderson now a "Chiantigiano" by adoption. However, some sustain that the word was coined at the end of the sixties, when the citizens of her Majesty the Queen first came here to discover a countryside similar to their own. Chiantishire was spoken of as if it were a place with a British calling, taste and style of living. The term is not very convincing even if it sounds right. The Chianti has always been and continues to be a Tuscan land, a land that preserves the style, traditions, tastes, and even the defects of the people who have always lived there. Nevertheless it is also true that it is probably the most multilingual countryside in the world. Therefore, if we really have to use the English language, why not call it Chianti country?

Market influences

Every Saturday, at the crack of dawn, the vendors of Greve Market crowd the elliptic shaped square and in a twinkling, between a witty crack and a naughty joke, they are ready to show their goods. The empathy and friendliness expressed by that Tuscan wit, the true Tuscan sense of humour, a destructive irony and a taste for a forceful word which does not sound too vulgar but rather becomes a means of arousing immediate consensus, are all natural talents which start from birth here and remain with you forever. Every day this itinerant market moves to various places in the territory: Radda, Castellina, Panzano, Gaiole, but the one in Greve is the largest and the most crowded. It is swarming with people, well disposed to buying even useless things, moving from stall to stall in the hope of finding something to buy. It's not like entering a shop to buy something you already had in mind. The market gives a sense of freedom and pleasure to those who have decided to dedicate a little time to themselves, accompanied by the agreeable and somewhat childish sensation of going to look for something which is waiting for us and will come to meet us but we don't have a clue what it is.

THE OLD URN

An old urn is cracked. It is in bad shape. It cannot be saved and must be chucked away, what a shame! Not here, it's enough for the broken object to arouse the slightest idea of being beautiful to look at, to get your imagination going so that the roundest and aesthetically most attractive part, where the belly of the urn curves and closes towards the mouth, for it to become a decorative ornament, at any rate something rare to be looked at. A small aesthetic sign abandoned in a neutral space. This may be exaggerated! Maybe!

In the parking lot of Castellina in Chianti, you leave your car. A wire netting surrounds a private property. There is an ugly roof and above it, the bottom of a broken urn. The roof continues to be a visually harsh note but the harmony brought by that piece of terracotta put there with apparent nonchalance, corroded and stained by the patient, inexorable, destructive effects of atmospheric agents, gives us the idea of a piece of pottery of other times which redeems the ugliness of the roof and gives us a choice of good taste in the art of creative recycling.

In the small villages, the market only comes once a week and this is why it is still considered a feast which satisfies all eyes and pockets. The products are very varied. You can go in famished and with nothing on and come out soon afterwards dressed to the hilt, having eaten your fill, washed down with a good glass of Chianti, generously offered in all the bars and wine-cellars.

The passion for woodworm

A journalist and writer, Giorgio Batini, still very active, who had taught me a great deal about the difficult profession of which he is an irrefutable master, wrote an intelligent book many years ago, with a witty, amusing title, which summed up, in an affectionate and charming way, a passion which appears a must in the lives of many Tuscans, namely that for antiques or old things. The book was entitled The *Dictionary of the Woodworm*, an enjoyable beginner's introduction to the secrets of collecting antiques. The publication was a success like so many of the works of the Florentine writer.

The title was even more so, seeing that the idea of a spiteful but familiar woodworm leaving its traces on a piece of furniture and also serving as a reliable proof of its age, was such a hit that many shops, especially small antique dealers and junk shops, exploited the idea of the woodworm for their business. The epidemic of this minute, harmless insect which did not present any risks, thus beca-

me chronic. In the large square in Greve, the authentic propelling centre of the village, two important events are held that are becoming more and more popular, one on Easter Monday and the other on the second Sunday in October. There are over one hundred stands of dealers from all over Italy with their fine antiques. We stop to touch an old Tuscan madia of a century ago, even if the restorer has been rather heavy-handed with it. Our pleasure grows in front of a rustic, chestnut table which undoubtedly welcomed a peasant family to their lunches and dinners. Then we come across a French sideboard, conceived and realised by a refined craftsman in the second half of the 18th century. There is also a fine table from Sorrento

with an incomparable intarsia effect which determines its taste and style: *The Vacanza Antiquaria* in Radda in Chianti is quite a different thing: It is an event which is distinguished by a better choice for a more demanding customer, twice a year, once at Easter and the other in September.

The Chianti... on a bike

You can see them advancing at a cruising pace, while small compact groups chat to one another with their eyes on the road. Suddenly they start up. There's a bit of excitement and the bikes swerve. A really fierce race is about to start among friends. Once it is over, they will take off their sports clothing and go back to their everyday sedentary lives. This race foresees a winner and a breathless bunch of losers. One of them shouts something to goad himself and his companions and is the first to be off. The others follow suit but things get tough as there's a sharp climb in front. They

all hang on tight to their bikes. The true test has arrived. The best of them go up easily. One of them has a healthy, wiry physique and can even be considered elegant with those muscles and the spirit of a climber. Others, a bundle of flab, soon give up as they don't have the drive. In the heat of the race, the group overtakes two young foreigners, also on their bikes but for entirely different reasons. They are a couple of tourists cycling along at quite a different speed. The difference is striking. The former are driven by a legendary sports tradition, while the latter are using their bikes as a means of transport over miles and miles, loaded with luggage, consisting of huge backpacks with sleeping bags, tents

and everything else that is required for heroic itineraries on two wheels without a motor. They are all young, almost all foreigners with a dream of going on a jorney in search of adventure and hardship.

Meeting a stranger

She doesn't seem to like our smile. It probably looks suspicious or maybe she's shy. We ask her if we can take her photo. She abruptly declines with a sharp, abrupt movement of her arm. She has no second thoughts about it. Pity, as she's a

beautiful, old lady. We met her near the church of San Cresci. She was sitting there in the cool, early spring sunshine in a black dress, black stockings, with dark wrinkles on her proud, motionless face. She stood there like an old woman now confined to a reserve, almost as if the changes of her countryside with elegantly renovated farmhouses, sophisticated shops and everything else had forced her to withdraw indignantly into her small, safe world, her house and the church. Both had always been there with her and her family: the former and the latter. The woman repeated her unfriendly gestures then pulled herself up moving towards the door of her truly peasant house, vanishing into her simple black and white life.

Artists in the Chianti

Many artists have returned in recent years to take up a more permanent residence in this area, in the hope of regaining a different sense of time. Seduced by the idea of putting themselves to the test in unfamiliar surroundings, many of them have chosen to settle there permanently. Others spend long periods alternating the slow rhythm of country life with the fast, chaotic but vital life of the city.

The pioneers

Allow me to go back to a fairly distant period in time, when my memory returns to two men, with different backgrounds and concepts about the world, but united by the same honesty towards their vocation.

I met the first many years ago and had to interview him. He received me in his isolated old farmhouse near Castellina in Chianti. He was sitting on a large stone, his wrists on his knees, his hands folded, his thoughts turned towards something grim. When he heard me coming, our eyes met as he was really gazing at me. He was Leo Ferré, the strolling actor and intellectual, the poet of the people who with his music, his sad, cutting songs, his bitter, passionate romances, had earned the fame of a troublesome individual, a man 'against'. He was frank, even harsh when necessary. He was always upset by the commonplaces of certain encounters, I realised that,

in his case, I had to leave the usual clichès behind me. He asked real questions and did not admit formalities. "Are you here to write that even Leo Ferré has chosen the Chianti, to live in this wonderful countryside which is still the most beautiful in the world, etc., etc, or are you here to speak to me?" I understood the provocation and the interview was a success and so was the meeting. A meeting that taught me something. Freedom for him was not something vague but a condition to be sought day after day. And to seek freedom you have to run more risks than usual and what is usual is not enough if you really want to run risks. Risk in itself implies a large amount of irresponsibility but also an ancestral link to the first instinct of life, so much so that the true risk of life is nothing but an impelling search, a useful anxiety besides being an act of generosity to yourself. This dimension of the soul was very much a part of himself. When we left, he said to me that the Chianti was very beautiful but the same could be said of many other parts of the countryside and that if he had bought a house here, it was because a friend had made him an offer and he had acted on impulse and, having done it, he had nothing to regret. We met again only once more before his death and now the memory of him is still strong.

His wife, signora Maria Christina Diaz Ferré and their daughter, Daniella, produce *Poggio ai Mori*, now an established Chianti Classico. They do this in that unassuming, practical way that Leo loved with the usual understatement.

During the same years, a friend of mine took me to a lovely farmhouse with a large garden full of local plants and a strange, inanimate vegetation. When getting closer to them, I realized that they were forged metal sculptures, hand-forged by the imaginative fantasy of Lionni who seemed in the past to have been an elegant professor of an English college behind whose sharp, bright eyes was hidden the soul of a child. And he confirmed this side of his nature when we got more familiar. Indeed, I had the sensation that I had come in touch with a current of child-like energy. Leo had already been affected by the disease that brought him to his death but

his playful dialogue with the world had not lost any of its freshness. We took leave of his imaginary plants (one of which can be admired in the square of Gaiole in Chianti) and we stopped at his studio to admire some canvases on which he was working and spoke about his activity as a writer and his main activity as a great advertizing artist and illustrator of children's books or also, as he suggested smiling, for "adults who refuse to grow up". And of course he considered himself the first of this category. Ferré and Lionni were among the first artists who, in less 'suspicious' times, loved this land.

Meeting at the bar

The bar is a public meeting place, usually the biggest of the village, where you can find a lot to eat and it is also the most popular centre where people meet in the afternoon to play scopa or briscola. This is not a habit, it has become a custom, something similar to a primary need. The people are of course the men of a certain age many of whom still wear their traditional felt hat with a brim, standing around a table with challenging eyes. One of them cracks a joke but the others don't seem to appreciate it. When you play, you play. When you play, you put your skills to the test. And that means a lot. This same tense atmosphere continues in the billiard room. Billiards is both sophisticated and popular. Nowadays it isn't so popular with young people but is still alive, at least for the limited circle of true enthusiasts. They are playing in the 'Italian' way. One of them plays with the coolness of an undisputed champion. He is about sixty. He has a thin, athletic figure, the hollow face of a smoker and the eternal cigarette in his mouth. He lives up to his image knowing that all eyes are fixed on him. Somebody lets out an unfortunate comment, one of those that makes the superstitious keep their fingers crossed. He just smiles while he prepares the cue rubbing it elegantly with the chalk. Then he bends down over the green table. He hits the ball, gains 180 points and wins. His adversary mutters under his breath because he was on the verge of defeating the local champion but didn't succeed in beating him, not even this time. The others applaud, resigned to defeat. The victor goes towards the bar to drink a glass to his own health and to that of the submissive admirers.

A theatrical festival

Gaia Bastreghi is above all an actress. She's one of those people capable of risking their own talents by dividing themselves between the traditional theatre and comedy, between the new Italian cinema, often with good ideas but almost always short of funds, and the opulent neurotic television screen. Gaia, like all true comedians, who belong to a species totally dedicated to the muses of the theatre, has in the meantime also discovered her strong leanings for organization. However, to be organizers in this difficult, stimulating job implies being capable of doing several jobs. Being an actor or also a director or, maybe, a careful observer of the changes of customs in the theatre and also an author. After having worked and lived in Rome for many years, she has been doing her own thing for the last two summers. She left her home and took up residence in the Chianti to be the artistic director of a festival which deserves our admiration and which will, in time, attract a much larger public. Thus we have the second edition of the *Festival del Chianti* which, thanks to the love of this actress-author-organizer, has gained international recognition. In the last edition, Lindsay Kemp danced and the director Hervé Ducroux brought his genius to a show of theatre and music presented in Radda in Chianti. The reasons for not letting the Chianti lose such an important cultural opportunity all exist. Now, those who administer the Chianti have the last word.

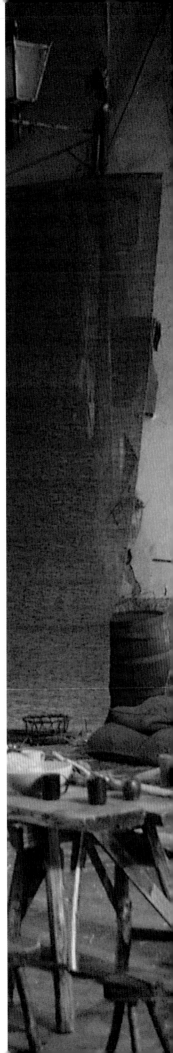

Cultured music in the vineyards

A few years ago, I had the pleasure of being invited to dine with a great conductor. He is one of those reserved, difficult men who live in a coherent, all-embracing relationship with their art; one of those who cannot bear compromises. Just because of this, he avoids them and when he has to deal with compromises he pretends not to understand. A talented conductor who after a life dedicated to music, during which he has directed important orchestras, also abroad, has decided to buy a delightful farmhouse hidden in the countryside of the neighbouring Florentine Chianti. Maestro Piero Bellugi organized a small group a few years ago and called it 'Orchestra of the Chianti'. He was assisted by his son David, a talented flutist who has taught for more than twenty years at the Florentine Music Academy. The orchestra made its first appearance... and was immediately successful. The concert was recorded and a CD was made for the future memory of a unique event. Strangely enough, nobody wanted to continue this courageous undertaking of Bellugi which had been created outside the complicated, pompous mechanisms of opera houses. Even if the project was a fiasco, it remains indelible in our memory. Now classical music is sponsored by funds from private sources and musical events of varying importance are organized independently. Among them, I wish to mention the concerts of San Polo in Rosso supported by music lovers. These concerts are sponsored by Katrin Canessa, the cultured owner of the splendid estate who surprises everybody by inviting famous musicians as her guests to San Polo in Rosso. This is also the case of the concerts organized on the farms Nittardi and Badia a Coltibuono, famous all over the world for their wines but also for the short musical season that they hold every year.

LE BARONE

A GLANCE OVER
THE CHIANTI COUNTRYSIDE

n one of the most charming areas of the region, where the ancient rival provinces of Florence and Siena mix into one, there is a pace of life soaked in beauty. Here we find ourselves guests at Villa Le Barone in the Chianti countryside close to the hilltop town of Panzano. This villa calls to mind the Central European atmosphere of Luchino Visconti's film, *Conversation Piece*, whilst still reminding us of the affectionate description that Aldo Palazzeschi made in his novel, *The Mattress Sisters*, regarding a Florentine villa that was home to an un-arrogant nobility. It is a villa with a beautiful rustic facade that has maintained its character and is able to boast belonging to the limited row of hotels that were the same even when the Chianti countryside still remained to be discovered. It is a welcoming building that remains faithful to the land, for better or for worse! And this belonging to the roots of the territory is apparent on first glance from the family air that exudes from the villa, the typical atmosphere of a beautiful countryside summer family home offering hospitality, but that remains essentially a private dwelling.

The customers, even though they are paying, are seen as "holiday-maker guests", as friends that are to be welcomed without apprehension, without affected ways or false pretences. Friends that spend their time relaxing in a place that has been little affected by fashions and new trends. As with many other buildings in the Chianti hills, Villa Le Barone also seems to have been built in the Middle Ages with the character of a defensive tower.

At the beginning of the fifteenth century the main body was enlarged and around the new building a Baron's farm was organised. Shortly afterwards the ownership passed on to one of the most renowned Florentine families, the Viviani della Robbia, and today, due to relative's rights, to the Aloisi de Larderel family. Around the building are English-style lawns with views over the countryside.

A privileged view point that dictates, in a quick gist, the entire natural nomenclature of the Chianti countryside.

And down there, right before our eyes, is the outline of a religious building of particular architectural importance, the Romanesque parish church of San Leolino, (named after he who was said to be the evangeliser of the Chianti countryside), which is adorned with a beautiful and incredibly well-preserved thirteenth century cloister.

Our stroll takes us into a small wood where tennis is being played and a group of children have gathered to chat.

But today I am a guest and an attendant indicates to me that lunch is served and is ready to distract me from these little visual delights. We eat outside, under the pergola, as though we were old friends.

We taste some dishes that follow our local traditions. There certainly is a type of magic here. Perhaps the magic of past times, tranquil and serene.

Podere Terreno or 'the art of hospitality'

We know some excellent agri-tourist farms in the Chianti, run by good friends but it's not up to us to praise one more than the other, as this is not a travel-guide to give information of the kind. Our aim is to describe impressions, pleasant experiences, encounters. Our meeting with Marie Sylvie Haniez and Roberto Melosi, owners of the agri-tourist farm Podere Terreno, situated on the road to Volpaia, in the municipality of Radda, was a fortunate one. Maybe because all three of us were in a good mood that day, so that the merit goes to the unfathomable and mysterious influence of the stars, or maybe because we were immediately on the same wavelength in our attitude towards life. That is, a direct approach but one full of subtle layers expressed in the way of small attentions. Without any formality but expressed with delicacy. I received from them, the sensation of not being welcomed as a duty but as an expression of

their natural vocation for hospitality – something extremely rare not only in the Chianti. Is this an exaggeration? I don't think so, it is what I really felt in the few hours spent with them after a day which ended with a dinner all around one table in the open air, eating delicious food accompanied by excellent wines produced on their small, select farm.

This is only the story of one encounter, as in the Chianti, the civilization of hospitality is well known and Sylvie's and Roberto's example is imitated by many other entrepreneurs, open to hospitality. They have all bought a property in the Chianti and have transformed their love for it into a job. But there are also castles, large villas and even privately owned abbeys, like Badia a Coltibuono where they offer a more refined accommodation. There is a vast choice therefore. A room or a small suite in a farmhouse or on a farm offers you more rustic surroundings whereas

the more elegant atmosphere of a 16th century villa is a choice for those looking for a more refined setting. A small monk's cell is more suited to those in search of 'privations', accompanied by all the comforts!

Chianti English style

Throughout Tuscany, and therefore throughout the Chianti, and more intensely so in the Chianti closer to Siena, the love for horses can be felt and seen. In the horse - breeding of the Berardenga, prize thoroughbred stallions and select broodmares are united in a marriage for money to bring potential champions to the turf into the world. There are numerous, well-managed riding-schools where half-breeds, a few old, quiet thoroughbreds, now physically on the wane, and several Maremmani no longer at the peak of their physical vigour, ride with 'neophytes' on the saddle. But the presence of horses here and there

in the countryside reveals that horse-riding is a common activity. Indeed, especially at week-ends, it is not difficult to come across small groups of people riding along one side of a road in the open countryside for a healthy gallop.

There is another very British sport too, though it has not caught on as a sport for the masses: golf. The club, ball, good arms, a lot of experience, a lot of self-control and a desire to walk over lawns as far as the eye can see. *The Golf dell'Ugolino* which we find at the very beginning of the Via Chiantigiana, as soon as we have left behind the last houses of Grassina and when the Chianti begins to appear with the first hills, is an appreciated structure which is now part of the Italian history of this ritual sport, having been opened a long time ago, in 1935. A large expanse of green hills scattered between Florence and the Florentine Chianti for the pleasure of all golf players.

Millemiglia

I came here specifically. I stopped the car near the curb of the road, just at the point where the political boundaries of the Chianti Classico end and the Val d'Elsa begins. A sort of border zone, also from the natural point of view; on one side the eye can see the last hills of the Chianti, on the other the first sunny lowlands of the Val d'Elsa. The circle of walls of Monteriggioni is only just a few hundred metres away, the broken rock of Staggia Senese is only a little further off, while San Gimignano, which pierces the sky with its thirteen bellicose towers, is perceptible to the eye or the imagination, down there, blurred on the horizon near the hills that rise at the end of a wide valley of vineyards and sunflowers.

The road that crosses this territory is the SS N2, the glorious, old road that, until a few years ago, everybody took to go from Florence to Siena and vice versa. Now the Superstrada has simplified the journey and accelerated the connections and the old road is not so busy as it is traversed only by a more disciplined local family traffic. But on this particular day in May, it is full of life. People have crowded the edge of the road looking towards Siena, people of all ages are waiting. We too have come here for the same reason. Everybody is there to see a parade of noisy cars which collectors define simply as 'vintage cars' but which are in reality legendary models, either with bodies that are too high or too flat or too long, in eccentric colours vibrating with passion. An epic of engines. It is the *Millemiglia*.

Browsing in the Chianti

From a brief journey on the web we have taken other... notes. Here they are:

chianti news.it

A magazine with everyday events, initiatives and services.

chianti.it

A periodical full of information and indications about food and wine.

chianticlassico.com

Official web-site of the Consortium with information on all the member farms, besides priceless advice on wine-tasting.

terreditoscana.regione.toscana.it

A well organized provider which gives information on Tuscan wines with details and charts on each wine. For connoisseurs.

adactanet.it/dominimusei

A well-prepared website which provides information on all the small museums of the Florentine Chianti, highlighting the more significant works with suitable, exhaustive comments. Only one black spot. Why only the paintings of the Florentine Chianti? A website for the true lovers of ancient art.

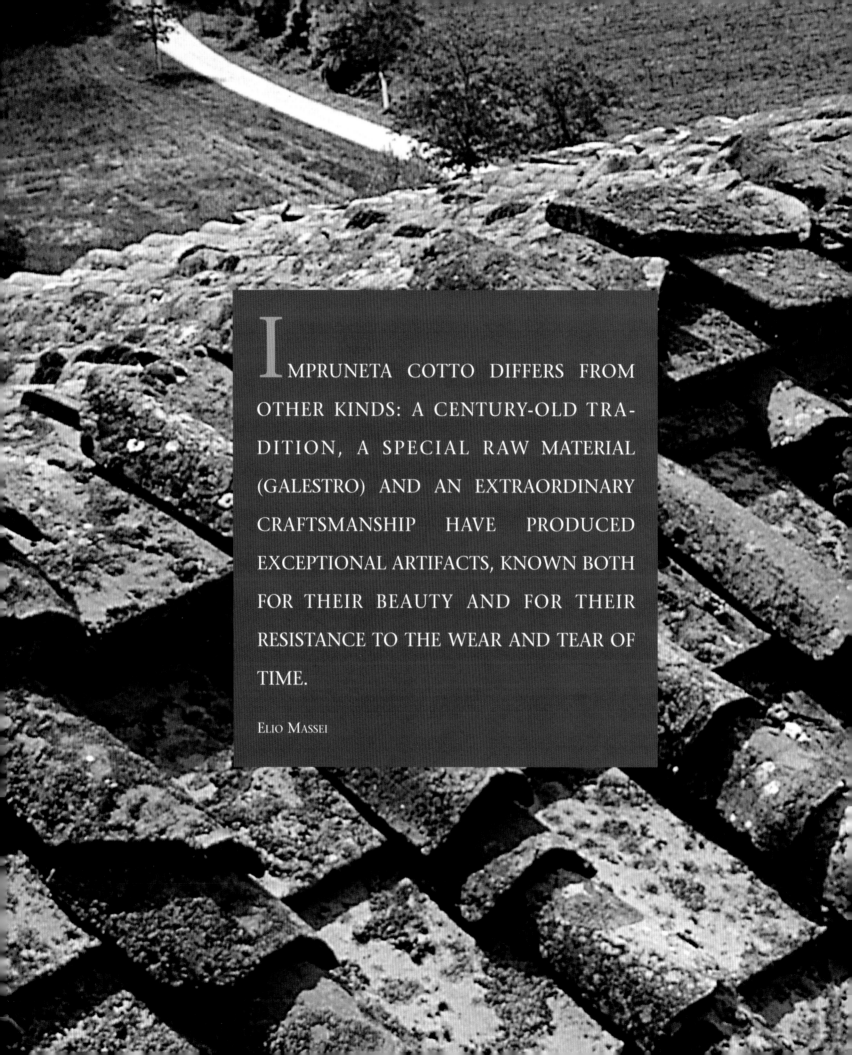

Impruneta cotto differs from other kinds: a century-old tradition, a special raw material (galestro) and an extraordinary craftsmanship have produced exceptional artifacts, known both for their beauty and for their resistance to the wear and tear of time.

Elio Massei

CRAFTS AND TRADES
COTTO AND OTHER PRODUCTS

COTTO
AND OTHER PRODUCTS

n the Chianti, it was necessary to be craftsmen from birth. This is no exaggeration but rather a condition imposed by living in the country in times when the inhabitants of the contado lived on the verge of poverty, making the mother of virtue a necessity. A consultation of the accurate study by Elio Massei specifically examines the local craftsmanship.

It informs us about its origins and growth.

It is no surprise therefore, when we discover that the early professional carpenters appear in the countryside only in the 19th century. Until the beginning of the following century, besides the blacksmiths who had always forged iron for different uses, the only craftsmen who did work for others were the coopers and cartwrights.

The former, skilful constructors and restorers of barrels, the latter, specialists in the construction of carts for agricultural work. Both trades were linked to the rural economy. Moreover, in the countryside, poverty prevented the growth of a relationship based on supply and demand. Indeed, the only customers financially capable of purchasing products directly from craftsmen were probably the landowners, those same owners of sumptuous palaces in Florence and Siena. But on the farms of the signori, which were closed, self-sufficient units, these craftsmen worked as smiths, joiners and carpenters because they were the jacks-of-all-trades living there on the spot and, when necessary, offered their services, compensated with food and lodging. They were often provided with workshops and small furnaces to bake tiles and bricks to be used for the rehabilitation and transformation of buildings included in the property.

Therefore, in the Chianti and all over the countryside, people were born craftsmen because they had to learn to produce the articles for their own household, starting from wood which had to be filed, carved and then transformed into functional, rustic everyday objects, simple beautiful chests which have now become rare and expesive, owing to an unstable market, subject to the changes of fashion. People have discovered the pleasure of having one of these simple pieces in their homes, without intarsia and carving, made in rough wood for practical reasons and not merely to please the eye. This furniture does not belong to any school or style and is appreciated for its essential beauty. This ancient, almost innate ability has, with time, led these craftsmen to put their century-old experience to good use. And now, the great grand-children of these craftsmen, accustomed to poverty, have finally turned their heritage into an asset by giving birth to trades which distinguish minor crafts, typical of the products of the Chianti. A familiar craftsmanship offers the delicate art of embroidery, straw articles or kitchen utensils obtained from olive and chestnut wood.

But ceramics and cotto are the crucial products on which the basics of the local handicraft economy is centred, the cotto of Impruneta and the Chianti.

The red cotto, which takes on more intense and severe tones in the Florentine and lighter and softer hues in the Sienese tradition is a daily reference point for Florentines, Sienese and Chiantigiani. Floors, tiled roofs, urns and pots, in short, what builders call 'round cotto'-

The Florentine earthenware

The great Florentine earthenware tradition has given

rise to veritable schools in aesthetics which, especially

from the 14th century onwards, predominate as models of

refinement and good taste. From the end of the

Quattrocento, the pottery masters of Montelupo produ-

ced magnificent articles for the Medici and the

Florentine noble families creating trilobate jugs, hand-

basins and plates with coats of arms, the decorations of

which, according to the Renaissance, consisted of rhom-

boid geometric figures enclosed in a circle. The main

colours were blue, green and orange. Later, the so-called

School of Cafaggiolo *where an indirect branch of the*

Medici family made a rare collection of precious porce-

lain, many pieces of which were coloured with that

incomparable turquoise, typical of many pieces of the col-

lection, was preferred to these beautiful works in pottery

from Montelupo. This school of pottery founded by the

Medici, was the first to be created in the western world.

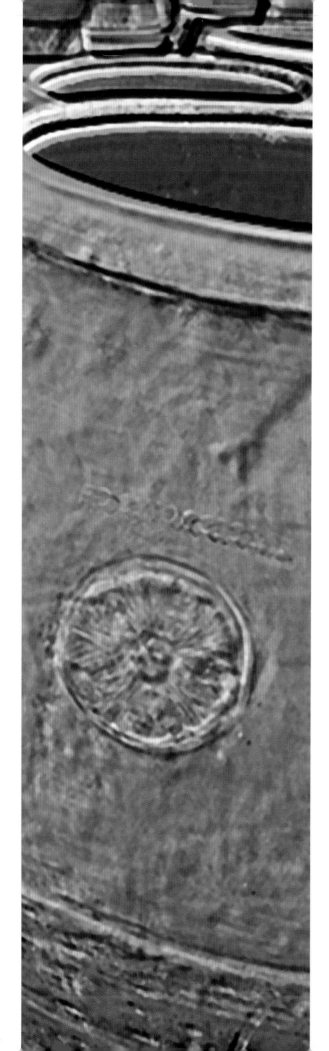

and 'square cotto' reveal their dual nature, constructive and decorative, in every village and every town. It can be seen on the floors of many Florentine and Sienese churches and libraries and on the rooftops that cover the most beautiful dwellings of Tuscany.

We wonder why a craft which is flourishing today, has developed in this particular area.

We will see that the first documents, showing the use of clay, date back to the 11th century: it marks the beginning of this tradition mainly in Impruneta but we should also say, in the Chianti, on condition that we identify the territory of those times as being the same geographic area as that of the present. But there is no doubt that this craft had already been employed for a long time. The craftsmen of cotto were first members of the guild of Doctors and Apothecaries and later, of Wine-makers.

In 1308, in Impruneta, the potters even united to form an independent guild, an evident sign of an activity that was already well established. In those times, it was the custom to serve wine in earthenware and in this area, wine has always been a faithful daily companion.

Milo Melani: The urns, 1967

THE JOURNEY

Using former techniques

Everywhere in the Chianti workshops can be found belonging to craftsmen who produce a very high quality of 'cotto' where each piece is unique, mainly because it is handmade.

At the Fornace di Campo al Sole, *near Radda in Chianti, the finest works we have seen are created in the same way as they were in an ancient work shop and where 'cotto tondo' and 'cotto quadro' are produced for all uses. The owner of Campo al Sole are true masters of this art and often collaborate with the Superintendence of Fine Arts for the restoration of floors and other decorations of ancient historical dwellings.*

The art of baking earth

My intention here is not to express disagreement. I shall limit myself to observing that the boundaries of the Chianti Classico were established purely for 'political' reasons. It has always been this way. Each contention needs a winner and the winner wants to gain the upper hand and to impose his own rules. This simple philosophical consideration wants to show that the reason why Impruneta was excluded from the prestigious itinerary of one of the most popular wines in the world was similar. Indeed, Impruneta is there, a stone's throw from the Chianti Classico area. Yet this small centre has not been included in the Chianti Classico in spite of its prestigious tradition. Through the centuries, Impruneta has succeeded in creating a famous make of cotto. Its furnaces have been the finest in existence for quite a few centuries so that when we refer to this ancient craft we say the 'cotto imprunetino', as if the noun and adjective had the meaning of one single word, suggesting that cotto that is not from Impruneta, is not cotto.

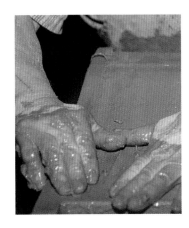

But Impruneta does not live only on cotto. It also includes the production of wine which is celebrated on the last Sunday of September with one of the first fairs dedicated to it, the *Feast of the Grape*, during which the inhabitants of the four quarters into which the village is divided, parade with allegorical carts celebrating wine, its symbols and its subjects. A few days later, during the week including the 18th of October, the day that celebrates the patron saint of this small town, there is another feast, this time as ancient as the origins of the village, the *Feast of San Luca*. These are the days of jubilation, a tangible sign of an authentic joy, of a deeply felt belonging to one's own traditions which are handed down from father to son. This is the feast of transhumance and livestock, but also the feast of wine and country life, an event which attracts large crowds and is organised as if it were something directly from the past, with games in the square and acrobats, horse races and big open-air dinners. The same feast that the brilliant artist Jacques Callot immortalized in a famous work in the first half of the 17th century. The artist had come to Florence in 1612 to perfect the difficult art of engraving and to work for the Medici family. His painting of the feast which transmits an atmosphere of light-hearted rural festivity, has always been much sought after by collectors all over the world.

The crafts of wood and straw

Baskets of different shapes and kinds crowd the entrance of a lovely Chianti shop, the Bottega dell'Artigianato which has always been situated at the end of the square in Greve. These rustic wicker baskets, finished with chestnut wood, the products for the kitchen made from gnarled olive wood and the small articles in dried, braided straw, are descendants of a great Florentine tradition known as the 'Straw of Florence'. At the end of the 19th and the beginning of the 20th century, it gave birth to a successful handicraft activity around Florence and in a part of the Chianti.

This craft has been replaced by manufactured products but there are still those who generously continue the tradition.

The last barrel-maker

"Silvano? Do you want to know where Silvano works? Take the road from Greve and follow the sign to Lamole. There, you will see a shed with a large number of barrels. That's where his hiding place is". It's a large shed full of wood, at the end of which you will find Silvano Batisti, the last barrel-maker of the Chianti. A survivor or rather the heir of a simple but precious craft, simple but difficult. He makes barrels and restores them but now, they say, he only restores them. He is a craftsman who has been learning the trade since childhood and has practised and improved it all his life. He may not have the sophistication of a more noble master who restores a painting on wood by a primitive artist but, seeing him work with such tireless zest, even now that he is threatening to withdraw from the limelight, arouses all our admiration. His grandfather, father, he himself and then, nothing. "In a few years I shall retire. This job ends with me. My children have no intention of continuing". Batisti has large, knotty arms and swings the two long hammers like an old gladiator whilst he replaces a short strip of wood from the barrel. Batisti who has a nose and taste for wine and all his senses tuned in with the noble nectar of the vines, defends the tradition of his ancient activity, expressing disapproval of barrels in other materials. As a wine lover ("but please don't say I'm an expert"), he admits he is not in tune with those in glass fibre which many firms have now adopted. "Wood, any kind, imparts its life to wine, synthetic barrels do not impart anything. Wine is a live product". Batisti is a simple man but this seems pure and moving poetry to us. Then he goes on to talk about the Chianti Classico wine. He says he does not want to talk about the choices that some producers make, "even if instinctively I can say it would be better to give the highest value to our products rather than cross them with foreign grapes. Chianti is made with a lot of Sangiovese and a little Canaiolo". Those who want to understand...

In the manner of Maniera

Maniera is a beautiful shop. Or rather, it is a large workshop with many masters who do not work but who meet here to show off their best products. It is as if they want to challenge each other, face-to-face or side-by-side, in a civilized but fierce match which does not necessarily require a winner and reminds us of the origins of a handicraft tradition of high standards. Naturally, this Tuscan tradition, which is still inspired by forms transmitted by ancient handicraft workshops, brings to the forefront that periods and styles and changes in taste do not exist when the result obtained goes well beyond a brief span of time. What this implies is that even today a plate of travertino, an elegant piece of pottery with archaic stylistic elements or a wrought iron bed entirely made by hand, can be extremely modern if made with the same manual skill of a thousand years ago. Daniela Tozzi Ryan, a pure Sienese, or as she defines herself, a 'Tuscan from Siena' which is an even more explicit way to point out her pride of belonging to her own roots, had a brilliant idea. It started from an authentic passion for everything that comes from manual work, followed by the necessity to find a new way, out of the ordinary, reminiscent of the past and different from anything one has ever seen. Not because of a maniacal search for originality but to pay homage to what she really loves. A shop, however refined and exclusive, would not be enough. We have to imagine a large showroom, a sort of permanent exhibition with objects for sale which are then replaced by others of the same kind but all different because they are sculpted and planed, wrought, stitched, turned by the hands of some of the most skilful craftsmen of Tuscany. They are the strange people who insist, against a trend going in other directions, on doing their job using the same techniques and with the same patience as their former masters. These master craftsmen are odd people who refuse to subject themselves to the power of technology, patient amanuenses who carry on the tradition of wood, iron, stone or pottery! Fortunately their "crazy" choice is fullproof against all temptations, as it is only thanks to their craft, often so similar to art, that they continue to keep alive the tangible signs of a civilization. So many precious materials require a space, but not any kind of space. This leads to another initiative pursued like a dream. In the same place where there used to be the kiln of the nearby Castello di Meleto, they are reconstructing a large building, starting from the ancient structure of the kiln, according to medieval forms and canons of construction. The difficult job is entrusted to the expert skilful hands of Architect Spartaco Mori, well-known in the Chianti for many restoration works. The result is something unique in the area, a stone building which is the biggest and most complex artifact on show at *Maniera*. But it is not for sale.

A shop... showroom

You can find ceramic plates, precious table linen, refined lace, earthenware pots, wooden bowls, rustic, emerald green glassware, brocades, glasses and wine jugs, rought iron beds and chairs... In this large suggestive showroom is a selection of the finest Tuscan craftsmanship.

Julia or 'the search for the beautiful'

To her friends she is Julia and also to others. Julia's surname is Scartozzoni but one has the sense that she is just Julia, because this is the idea she has of herself, that of being a friend to herself and to the world. One day Julia started to paint but then it wasn't enough for her, so she became interested in the restructuring of interiors and began an activity which did not exist in traditional professions. It was the result of her own creative imagination. It is not surprising therefore that we see her in the role of a refined craftswoman painting materials and precious fabrics, almost always with floral patterns in a fine style. Immediately afterwards, we see her taking a wad and sketching an initial idea for an interior decoration on which she is working. Julia is a designer, meaning that she is a woman with a marked personal taste, a versatile personality. Until a few years ago, she was also a talented *chef* and in this field too, she applied her inquisitive and imaginative inclinations, thanks to which she added a different touch to even the most traditional Tuscan dishes.

Her small farmhouse in Borgo Argenina, a hamlet near Monti in Chianti, is a jewel. It is the most beautiful present she has given herself. It is impregnated with the taste of a woman who needs to make her overflowing vitality felt through a colourful, rich style. Her studio, on the contrary, in the old barn, is more harmonious, with a sophisticated sense for the essential. When she receives her guests at home, she communicates her femininity with a warm, cosy and somewhat coquettish interior. When she enters her studio, she tries to be less like Julia and more open to others. We can imagine her alone in her studio with the big table, tubes of acrylic paint and a terrace with large window panes looking onto the Chianti, painting fabrics and planning the interiors of farmhouses in the same spirit as those who are trying to grasp something they do not yet understand but that is already deep down inside them, something lively and elusive like her life that never stands still.

THE CHIANTI IS FULL OF SMALL LANDOWNERS, NEITHER RICH NOR POOR, WHO LIVE ON WHEAT, WINE AND SILK... AND ACORNS FOR THE LARGE NUMBER OF PIGS; THERE IS ALSO OLIVE OIL AS WELL AS MANY CHESTNUT FORESTS ON THE MOUNTAINS WITH NUMEROUS PASTURES IN THE WOODS, ESPECIALLY IN SPRING AND SUMMER FOR THE COWS AND THE SHEEP.

PIETRO LEOPOLDO, GRAND-DUKE OF TUSCANY

THE ART OF SIMPLE COOKING

EATING IN THE CHIANTI

EATING IN THE CHIANTI

hen eating enough wasn't a certainty but only a possibility, the talent of cooking new dishes with the leftovers was perfected almost to a fine art. In this way, they solved two requirements, using up the bits of what was produced by the sweat of the brow and doing something to please God Almighty who would not put up with any waste of food. He donates to us through nature. In other words, the *chef*, the creative source of inspiration at the basis of all cookery that makes a virtue of need, was poverty. In this area too, the cooking has been applied and adopted to combine the necessity of limited expenses with the natural search for results to satisfy the smell, the taste and that nondescript something that we call the soul.

Now, everything has changed radically, but the tradition of those simple dishes is alive, carried on with dignity by the women of local families or, at least, by those who are part of a rapidly changing society but do not want to lose this rich heritage belonging to the culture of food and therefore to the civilization of the usage and customs of a society that claims the right to be defined as such.

On examining an ideal menu, created by the people of the Chianti, we can come across unforgettable encounters with rich vegetable soups, cooked on a low flame with some chopped vegetables, the 'battuto' and a lot of experience; we shall have the joy of seeing a fine array of soups which includes an indisputable winner at the top of the list, the famous 'ribollita'. Eaten the day after, this bread soup tastes even better. Then there is the 'pappa al pomodoro' tasting and smelling of basil, garlic and tomato and, also, 'panzanella', a choice peasant dish which testifies to what we have just said, seeing that bread that had been left over for a few days and had got too dry, was soaked, squeezed and seasoned with salt, basil, onions and tomatoes. An extremely simple, tasty dish still served in the same way today, perhaps with the addition of a few vegetables, so as to give us the idea that we no longer live in the same straitened circumstances. The staple of all these dishes is bread, which in Tuscany is prepared without salt, in long, round or square loaves, baked in a wood oven when possible and always excellent but certainly better eaten the day after. Once the good smell of fresh bread has gone, the taste is even better, like a full-bodied wine that needs to be opened several hours before drinking, to reveal its personality.

Bread is also the main ingredient in the 'fettunta': bread toasted over the embers, rubbed, still hot, with a clove of garlic and a drop of oil to enhance the taste of unsalted bread and this simple masterpiece is ready to be sacrificed to any famished mouth.

The 'insaccati', the cured ham and salami are among the most tasty in Italy. Meat dishes are not numerous but are the 'forte' of all good cuisine. Then, there is a vast choice of beef, pork, lamb, grilled or cooked in baking hot ovens or on the flame for our delight.

THE JOURNEY

Preserving homemade cooking

During this journey, we stopped to examine the proposals of some famous restaurants which had been recommended to us, but for detailed indications, the reader is advised to look at the notes at the end of this book. It is not our intention to express an opinion, by approving or criticizing, but rather, we shall try to give our impressions which, being personal, must be taken merely as an opinion. Having stated this, it is natural for us to say

creativity of a master chef would be superfluous.

This is the case of *La Bottega di Volpaia*, a small restaurant with just a few tables, a friendly atmosphere not giving any importance to refinements, where the cook serves those who happen to be there, offering the same dish from the same pot or pan, from which he serves himself and the other members of his family. The cooks are Carla and Gina Barucci who were born in the small

that we do not eat well everywhere in the Chianti. In recent years, catering has increased enormously, maybe excessively. Those who want to discover the taste of the local cooking, should give priority to some of the small family-run trattorie. Perhaps it would be more accurate to call them 'resting points with cooking facilities'. They are informal places where the idea of adding something new to the dishes of our great great grandparents does not even occur to them the

hamlet of Volpaia and will remain there for the rest of their lives.

"I've put a really good meal on my stomach"– says a young American while she hands over some money to the owner, as a paying guest. Her friend agrees and she insists: "Yes, it was a really good meal" not knowing that with her inaccurate Italian, she has just used a popular Florentine expression of the ancient nobility. The word 'eating' should be interpreted as food while

the expression 'on the stomach', instead of the more correct one 'into the stomach' is very typical. 'On my' is something you feel, which continues to give you a passing joy of being full till the time of digestion but which is not heavy and makes you cheerful. We get close to her glancing at the bill and find out that that good food is 'ribollita' which they really cook well here. But the experience of this place is the same as many others with cooking facilities, found here and there in the area as a pleasant alternative to more sophisticated restaurants.

The Antica Macelleria

Falorni

The Falorni Family has

remained here in the

same building, since the

end of the 18th century.

It is a true 'boutique'

for those who like meat

and salame, well-known

all over the world for

the high quality of its

products.

The ladies of another kind of catering

Who can understand, by nature, the art of hospitality better than a woman? Travelling around the Chianti, one of the things that strikes you, is the presence of women entrepreneurs, especially in the field of catering. But, as we all know, the creativity of women can not be bound in chains. Consequently some of them have invented a successful, imaginative cocktail, based on instinct, a 'healthy' practical sense and enthusiasm. They invented a job which unites the art of catering to that of hospitality. Some owners of important historical dwellings offered their services as cookery experts, organising private courses for a few days on their ancient, hospitable estates. These are true lessons in the art of cooking where the participants, as in a progressive English boarding school for adults, visit the Chianti, help in the kitchen, learn the secrets of their teachers and then go home, satisfied, having learnt something new which they will soon put to good use.

The 'mastro beccaio' of Panzano

There is no doubt about it. The Chianti is a place with good butchers. Some even excellent. But it is not the only place where you find good butchers. This is to do justice to all those masters in butchery who are not so fortunate as to have a shop in this place.

The Chianti is a noble territory and the success it enjoys belongs to it by right. It is also fortunate because everything that is begun here immediately acquires a sense of exclusiveness, typical of trendy places. Let us enter a famous butcher's shop. The 'master butcher', or in other words, the present butcher complains about being disturbed by a BBC troupe who have just asked permission to shoot a film. But the butcher of Panzano does not appreciate anything impromptu: "You should first have telephoned me, fixed an appointment and I would have been at your disposal. As things are, I feel like an animal in a cage." Oh yes! Tuscans are inflexible and they know what they want. We understood that this is the welcome we too would have got, so we tried to explain the reason for our visit. He fixed an appointment and we returned the next day.

In the midst of sirloin steaks and salami, lard and small aromatic meat balls, ready to be put into a frying pan, Dario Cecchini, a connoisseur of food and art, revolves around his world like a typhoon who gets rid of everything so as to focus all attention on himself. He serves the elderly customer next door who probably knew him from childhood and who is as witty as he is, beginning a quick-witted verbal duet with her. At the same time, he argues on the phone with somebody he doesn't agree with and, meanwhile, he grasps the doubts of a new customer and answers his tacit question without the former being able to get a

The "mastri beccai of the Chianti"

The art of butchery is deeply felt. Indeed, we could say that each area is proud of having its own 'master butcher'. Among the numerous Chianti specialities, can be enjoyed hams and salami from the 'Sienese cinta', which can be distinguished by the exceptionally strong taste and smell.

Pecorino from the Chianti

or better, from Tuscany

In his 'Historia Naturalis', Plinius
had already mentioned Tuscan pecori-
no as a delicacy even if he referred to
that produced in Luni. A dairy pro-
duct of Etruscan origin, this cheese
has been one of the typical products
of Tuscan gastronomy for more than
two thousand years. In 1986, the
regulations for controlling the origin
of a product, DOC, were established.
Today, its production is controlled by
the Consortium with the same name
which promotes its image throughout
the world.

word in edgewise. When he ultimately dedicates his attention to us, he becomes an experienced actor. He puts on a panama hat, takes a sharp knife and recites the XXXIII Canto of Dante's *Inferno*, that of Conte Ugolino. He has a stentorian voice coming from his diaphragm as is taught in acting schools and he knows it all by heart according to the most classical Tuscan tradition. He is almost as good at it as Benigni, but like him, there are many others, just as talented because in the small Tuscan centres, the pride of belonging to the same origin as the great poet of the *Divine Comedy*, is still alive.

He still has time to talk about cooking and cooking traditions. He lets us into some of his secrets and refers to his website where some of his recipes can be found.

The square of Panzano, surrounded by houses, is small and quiet. We have now made friends with Dario and have discovered a mutual passion for music. The silence is interrupted for a few moments by *Confutatis Maledictis* from Wolfgang Mozart's *Requiem* which our new friend turns up at full volume to welcome us. That music puts us on the same wavelength. We don't know if a group of tourists, surprised by these notes which thunder like divine justice, feel the same emotion.

Sheep and pecorino

A building without any character and with a hand-written signboard in two languages. Typical local cheese for sale: Cheese Schafskäse. This is the only simple, commercial reminder by a shepherd, not the only one in the Chianti. His sheep graze on the top of a hill behind which, on the horizon, we can see a row of cypresses. The sheep, crowded together like a single, dirty white ball, the cypresses and the horizon lit by the sun are the image of an irritating, stereotyped beauty, like those you accidentally come across everyday and pretend

not to see. The protagonists are so obvious and the context so normal that to lose self-control would mean, to lower the level of your self-esteem. But, fortunately for us, our sensitive friend is more aware of the beauty of the landscape than personal pride. It is in this very same part of the Chianti that the great Tuscan cheese makes its entrance as a protagonist, in an area near Siena which is more suitable for sheep pasture. This Tuscan pecorino, in all its forms, preserves its fragrance and taste everywhere in the region, thus becoming the most delicate of Italian pecorinos. The fresh kind is agreeably delicate but the more seasoned one is just as delicate and, if anything, more tasty. The best kinds can be found in the valleys of Arbia and Orcia where Pienza, that crazy Renaissance example of the ideal city, born from the pride of a Pope and the mind of a brilliant architect, welcomes us with its rare beauty to give us advice about the best Tuscan pecorino.

The Chianina thoroughbred

They have placid, wide open eyes. The white coat of the Chianina breed emphasises its stocky build, outlines the thick bone structure, the protruding tendons. They are among the biggest cows in the world and come from afar, ever since the 2nd –3rd centuries BC, when they were used by the Etruscans for food and to till the fields. The Chianina oxen are one of the recurring themes of so many rural paintings by the great Macchiaioli masters. The painters, the most famous of whom is Giovanni Fattori, painted in the open fields, fine gardens, the suburbs of cities, depicting the emotions inspired by their surroundings. More than one century ago, it was much easier to come across these big, peaceful cows at pasture than it is today. For this is the meat that has given life to the noble tradition of 'la fiorentina' (the Florentine beefsteak), probably the most famous dish of our cuisine. A piece of meat, 3 or 4 centimetres thick, weighing no less than one kilo, grilled on the embers for a few minutes (the meat must be rare), without adding salt or oil, ready to absorb the aromas of the flame and to enhance their own. It must be salted only after cooking. Some add a drop of raw olive oil, the choice should be left to individual taste.

In actual fact, the beefsteaks were once more appropriately called 'carbonate' (cooked on the flame). It is difficult to say when the word changed. The story is the following, but it is probably only a story. It happened in Florence in the 16th century, in the small streets next to the Basilica of San Lorenzo. There was a feast dedicated to San Lorenzo, one of the patron saints of Florence. The carcass of an ox, naturally of the Chianina breed, was turning on the spit. In a foreign language could be heard, in the midst of the crowd, "beefsteak, please!". They were the voices of some English merchants, drawn by that succulent sight. As there have always been good relations between the Florentines and the British, it seems that the old word 'carbonata' was gradually abandoned and replaced by the Anglo-Saxon beefsteak.

A pig worthy of a painting

A bit of simple ethology was offered by a really competent friend of ours who told us in truly affectionate tones, about the generous character and exquisite meat of a breed of pigs, the secular pride of Siena and the Chianti, the 'Cinta' (this word is found in several Tuscan dialects meaning belt or collar), that is, a pig with fine loins, whose pure breed is preserved by a few breeders with the same attention with which the proud inhabitants of the city of the Palio preserve the standards of their 'contrade'. The 'cinta' is a much lighter animal than most of its breed and still sufficiently wild to require fairly extensive spaces in which to move freely. It has the long, fierce snout of the wild boar with which it shares an obvious kinship and compensates all this attention by sacrificing itself for the pleasure of us humans in savoury dishes, ham and salami with a special taste of wild game. It belonged to an ancient breed, a very ancient one. In a masterpiece of early Tuscan art, can be seen an example of the prize pig climbing up a low rock, followed by a young peasant. It belongs to the fine cycle of frescos entitled *The Effects of Good and Bad Governance* that Ambrogio Lorenzetti painted in an affectionate and reliable style in the 'Sala dei Nove' of the Palazzo Pubblico in Siena from 1337-1339.

SUGGESTED RECIPES

SALAD WITH RAVEGGIOLO AND RICOTTA

FRESH FRUIT SALAD WITH ZUCCOTTO AND BAVAROISES

PANZANELLA

STEWED RABBIT

HOMEMADE TAGLIATELLE

JULIA'S RECIPES

In another part of the journey, we talked about Julia as a designer.
Instead, in this context, we want to introduce her as the skilful custodian
of Tuscan culinary traditions. We were enjoying our meal as her guests.
We asked her to reveal those secret recipes that we had just tried.
She was delighted to do so, seeing that a few years ago, she had been
an appreciated chef.

SALAD WITH RAVEGGIOLO
AND RICOTTA

*"This dish is simple to prepare but requires fresh ingredients, from the
cheese to the vegetables.Arrange the rocket mixed with seasonal salad on
each plate.In the centre, place some raveggiolo and put small tomatoes all
around it, pieces of ricotta and strips of raw courgettes obtained by using a
potato peeler. Lastly, season the salad with salt, a little ground pepper
and olive oil".*

FRESH FRUIT SALAD
WITH ZUCCOTTO AND BAVAROISES

"When preparing the bavaroises, it is preferable to use seasonal fruit and you can choose figs, strawberries, red grapes, peaches, plums or kiwis, taking into consideration that the quantity necessary for four portions is 250 g of fruit, whatever it happens to be. For 4 moulds, 250 g of fruit, are required about 125 g of sugar, half a lemon, 2 sticks of jelly and 250 g of cream.

After having washed and peeled the fruit, mash it and add the sugar and the strained lemon juice. Then soak the jelly in cold water, squeeze it and let it melt in a pot on a very low flame. Meanwhile, whip the cream, and when the jelly, now liquid, has cooled down, delicately stir before mixing it with the fruit purée and then with the whipped cream. Lastly, pour the mixture into small moulds and put it all in the refrigerator for at least 4 hours. When you are preparing the dish, take the bavaroises out of the moulds by placing them in hot water for a few seconds and, lastly, decorate them with the fruit used for the purée".

ZUCCOTTO

"To prepare the zuccotto you need 200 g of sponge cake cut into thin slices, 220 ml of fresh cream, 300 g of cow's milk ricotta, 50 g of black chocolate, the same quantity of candied fruit, 130 g of icing sugar, bitter cocoa and 100 ml of Alchermes. First, whip the cream with the sugar, stir it with the ricotta and divide it into two parts. In one, mix the cocoa, in the other, the candied fruit and the chocolate chopped into pieces. Now put the slices of sponge cake into a bowl with the liqueur, mixed with 3 tablespoons of water, then line a medium-sized, smooth, deep bowl with a few slices of sponge cake remembering to leave a few for the bottom of the cake. Lastly, pour the white mixture, followed by the cocoa pressing it slightly down to fill the empty spaces. Finish with the sponge cake set aside and put in the fridge for a few hours before serving".

RITA'S RECIPES

Rita Marini is a young woman from the Chianti who cooks following the traditions of her birthplace. At a dinner of a mutual friend, we tried some of her excellent recipes which we would like to present.

PANZANELLA

"Panzanella is a quick refreshing summer dish invented by the peasants to use up the bread, left over even a week before. The recipe is very easy to follow but is also very gratifying if prepared in the right way.

For 4 people, soak 400 g of stale Tuscan bread in cold water. Then squeeze it well with your hands but not too much and mash it in a bowl. Now add two ripe, red tomatoes cut into thin slices, 1 medium cucumber cut into thin slices and a medium, red onion, roughly chopped and left to soak in a few tablespoons of red vinegar for 15-20 minutes. Lastly, add 6-7 leaves of chopped basil and, after having seasoned with oil, vinegar and salt, mix well and put the panzanella into the refrigerator until serving".

STEWED RABBIT

"Stewed rabbit once used to be a special dish, prepared on feast days when the women, free from other commitments, could devote more time to cooking. The recipe isn't difficult but requires a certain amount of attention and patience. Take a rabbit of about 1 kg and chop it into pieces. After having washed it, put it into a pan together with the liver, and let it simmer. Gradually drain the water until the rabbit is almost dry. Now add the olive oil, a few sprigs of rosemary, raise the flame and cook it until it has turned brown. Now, remove the liver and put it on one side. Then add 1 carrot, 2 ribs of celery and two tufts of parsley, all chopped finely together and let it simmer for 2-3 minutes. After a while, add the chopped liver, half a glass of red wine, salt and pepper. Lastly, when the wine has evaporated, pour 4-5 tablespoons of tomato purée and let it cook on a low flame for about 2 hours".

HOMEMADE TAGLIATELLE

"While the rabbit is cooking, prepare the tagliatelle using 300 g of plain flour, 3 fresh eggs and a pinch of salt. First, put the flour on a smooth surface, forming a hole into which you break the eggs and add the salt. Then, using a fork, blend the ingredients and when the eggs are well mixed with the flour, add a tablespoon of oil to make the dough more elastic.Continue to knead the dough briskly then, after 7-8 minutes, roll it into a ball and let it rest in a cool place, covered with a cloth for about 15 minutes. At this point, roll out the pasta with a rolling pin, forming a thin, rectangular sheet which must then be rolled up. Lastly, cut the roll into slices and put the tagliatelle on a kitchen cloth, slightly sprinkled with flour".

WINE IS THE BLOOD OF THE EARTH,
THE SUN CAPTURED AND TRANSFORMED
BY SUCH AN ARTIFICIAL STRUCTURE AS THE
GRAPE, A WONDERFUL LABORATORY, WHERE
MACHINERY, INTELLIGENCE AND ENERGY
ARE PUT TOGETHER BY A PERFECT MAGICIAN
SORCERER AND THE WINE IS TRANSFORMED
INTO A MASTERLY COMPOUND OF SAP AND
LIGHT, THANKS TO WHICH HUMAN
INVENTIVENESS EMERGES DISTINCTLY AND
CLEARLY, THE SOUL EXPANDS, THE SPIRIT IS
COMFORTED AND HILARITY REIGNS SUPREME.

GALILEO GALILEI

VINEYARDS AND OLIVE GROVES

THE COUNTRYSIDE BETWEEN BUSINESS AND PASSION

THE COUNTRYSIDE
BETWEEN BUSINESS AND PASSION

iuseppina Strepponi, Verdi's devout lifetime companion and muse had sacrificed her own career at the peak of her success as a soprano for the genius of Busseto. In a few lines written to a friend, she revealed an unusual and unexpected side of her famous companion's character. That great man whom historians described as a gruff and withdrawn personality, showed other more sensitive aspects of his character in his private life.
"Verdi – she wrote – is well, has a good appetite, runs around the garden, sleeps and drinks Chianti, nothing but Chianti. Long live Chianti and those who succeeded in obtaining such a good one."
Now, it is well known that Verdi ate and drank with gusto. It is more difficult to imagine the sanguine and proud creator of *Othello* and *La Traviata* running lightheartedly, much like a child, on his lawn. However as we do not want to deny that tender observation it is natural to suppose that the newly found desire to… frolic was aroused by a few extra glasses of Chianti which Verdi preferred to any other wine. Verdi who was born in the area of the Lambruschi and Trebbiani.
This was Verdi. But how many great men probably favoured the nectar of these vines? Michelangelo is another artist who loved wine. Indeed, he seems to have been the owner of a 'casa da oste' which in those times meant a rustic villa. A letter to his nephew Lionardo, written on 19th April 1549, testifies his firm intention to purchase a house in this area. The artist writes: *"I prefer to buy that farm in the Chianti rather than keep the money"*. That farm is probably the present one called Nittardi, situated in the countryside of Castellina. It is a small wine producing farm and has been one of the most popular in the area for some time. Michelangelo who was by then getting on in age, seems to have gone to this property to control the harvest personally and to produce a wine which he obviously sustained as being the best in the Chianti. He made a precious gift of this wine to the Pope or Popes, seeing that there had been at least four Popes in the last fourteen years of his life. After him, many famous men have had dealings with the Chianti. This time we can rely on a vast documentation. A faithful student and friend of Galileo Galilei, Vincenzo Viviani, informs us that

the scientist who shook the ancient, obtuse astronomical certainties and paid dearly for it, owned a farm near Grignano. As a wine grower he seems also to have given vent to his natural thirst for knowledge, trying out new grafts and personal innovations.

However, Galileo was also a poet, one of those rare men, able to grasp the strength of an emotion and express it in words. As a poet, he probably wrote the most touching lines dedicated to wine: *"Wine is the blood of the earth, the sun captured and transformed by such an artificial structure as the grape, a wonderful laboratory, where machinery, intelligence and energy are put together by a perfect magician-sorcerer and the wine is transformed into a masterly compound of sap and light thanks to which human inventiveness emerges distinctly and clearly, the soul expands, the spirit is comforted and hilarity reigns supreme".* It is the concept of a scientist and man of faith who fells the presence of God as *"the perfect magician-sorcerer"* who has planned everything in nature; a God who can be found in everything that exists and hence also in that *"wonderful laboratory"* that is, the grape which gives birth to wine, *"a liquor of great art composed of sap and light".*

Chianti used to be… white!

The documented history of Chianti has been recorded for many centuries, whereas the 'unofficial' one began… at the origin of life on the planet, as fossils of *vitis vinifera*, several million years old, have been traced in Tuscany. We also know that the Etruscans and the Romans drank wine and that after the fall of the most glorious Empire of all times, during the dark ages of the Barbarians, the age of destruction and chaos, the monks took refuge in their impregnable abbeys with the impelling desire to save the memory of the longest and most prolific period of civilization from the obscurity of violence. They started to write down everything they knew, with the patience, the accuracy and the humble skilfulness of those who are not seduced by the bad advice of haste as they had a very personal concept of time in their lives. Furthermore, they also wrote about how the land and the vines had been cultivated until then. This was also recorded in accurately documented texts by the monks of Badia a Coltibuono and Badia a

133

Passignano, texts which certainly contributed to the diffusion of viticulture in this area.

The actual history began in 913. A parchment, found in the church of Santa Maria a Lucignano, describes the practice of wine making in the Chianti. From then on, there is a continuous increase of evidence. The Guild of vintners was established in the second half of the 13th century and it is well known that in Florence, Siena and other cities, inns and wine cellars were opened where people could drink and make merry. The wines were *red and sparkling*. There was not yet any mention of Chianti. It was necessary to wait until a commercial contract was signed in 1398 by Ser Lapo Mazzei, a literary man, jurist and scholar of economics in the service of the Florentine Signoria. Ser Mazzei authorises the payment for *"6 barrels…of white Chianti wine"*. Here comes the surprise. In those times, the word Chianti meant a white wine produced in the territory of the present Sienese Chianti. In the present-day Florentine Chianti, which was not yet included in the area, red wines were produced. Some of the most popular were those of Valdigreve, Vignamaggio, Montefioralle and Uzzano. In his *Commentary to the Divine Comedy* in 1481, Landino says that *"the valley of the Chianti produces excellent wine"*. It is nevertheless difficult to establish when the Chianti changed its colour and was identified as a red wine. At the beginning of the 18th century, in the times of Grand Duke Cosimo III de' Medici, Chianti wine had already become very famous, to the point that they decided to establish the geographic boundaries of the area of production which has remained the same as that of today, except for a few slight differences. A ministerial decree of 1932 went further, by differentiating the Chianti wine produced in the territory of the same name from the Chianti wine produced in the other areas of the Florentine province, thus stressing the special qualities of the former.

Chianti Classico… for purity!

I've always been passionately interested in wine, to the point of feeling I have absorbed into my sense of smell and taste, the memories which are commonly known today as 'information', necessary to understand if a wine is well made or has suffered, if it has been 'stripped' too much or if it has been served slightly 'chiuso', a term denoting a wine, which not having had enough time to be exposed to air, has not been able to express its best qualities and characteristics. I'm even able now to recognize, with an acceptable margin of error, whether the wine I'm

The most beautiful cellar of the Chianti Classico

You need a lot of imagination. Although this is a fine photograph, it cannot create the exact atmosphere you breathe when you enter the cellar of Monsanto. Have we entered a secret passage of the castle, once used by the Signori to escape from danger? Are we in a secret passageway of a monastery leading to the doors of penitence and expiation? No, we have simply entered the largest cellar ever seen for maturing wine. It is more than 200 metres long beneath the walls of the large fortified complex. What is even more extraordinary is that this cellar is not ancient but the result of Fabrizio Bianchi's and his daughter Laura's passion for wine. They had it built fairly recently, following the philology of ancient building canons. Outside, is the park and the vineyards which produce, among other wines, the much appreciated Chianti Classico 'Il Poggio', a remarkable red wine, greatly admired by the most critical judges. It is a farm offering a personal form of hospitality and an innate savoir faire.

drinking is a pure Sangiovese or whether it presents a higher or lower quantity of Cabernet or other grapes. But a true expert, one of those who understands wine immediately or who suggests crossbreeding and the harmonious blending of grapes, one with a 'nose for wine' and a strong sense of taste, is a very rare man, much sought after in the land of wines. The aforementioned person is a natural oenologist, the true trump card for all producers today. It seems to me that the oenologists who work for the Chianti can be divided into two schools of thought, incompatible with one another. The protectionist school prefers to try and improve more and more, if possible, the yield and characteristics of home grown grapes, those that have represented the wines of the Chianti Classico since time immemorial. The other, more attracted by innovation, without neglecting tradition, seems to be more interested in creating new wines, alternatives to the Chianti Classico. Nothing wrong with this! But the predominant school is the one that promotes the idea of obtaining as much as possible from the home grown grapes of the Chianti. One of this group is Alessandro Alì, an oenologist and wine expert with whom we exchange opinions on the subject.

Alì is a defender of the faith in favour of tradition, a tradition which many are trying to further improve with the precise conviction that from Sangiovese, a fine quality, but somewhat hard grape, whose qualities are difficult to exploit to a maximum, better results can still be obtained. "We should study" says Alessandro Alì "as many already do, the characteristics of the vineyard and its interactions with the climatic and paedological environment, as well as a series of cultivation practices which I shall not touch upon here.

I should like to see various French grapes like Cabernet Sauvignon and Merlot emplo-

yed above all in important fashionable wines which have been given names such as Supertuscan, thus leaving the Tuscan stage free for King Sangiovese. Even if we use grapes for improvement or as alternatives, it is necessary to consider the explosive influences, the mildness and strength, on the typical austerity of Chianti Classico. It is true that this is the new trend, but we have to work towards softening Sangiovese, the most important and typical element of the Chianti Classico".

The 'adjectives of wine'

The adjectives worthy of the best of D'Annunzio are those used, or better, conceived to describe wine. Cultured, elegant, literary adjectives which go beyond the limits of an objective description, suggesting a 'creative' key which further ennobles an already noble drink. It is here then, among the numerous technical charts we have read in the most famous wine producing farms, that we have found this special, at times excessively free dictionary of adjectives chosen to describe the characteristics, qualities and distinguishing features of each individual wine.

When a wine is new, the colour could be almost scarlet with purple hues; when it is only young, it will usually be a cherry-red; when it remains in the barrel for average ageing, it becomes an orange-red. Instead, when it has matured for more than two years, it turns a brownish red. But things get complicated when we talk about the bouquet. It is here that literary adjectives which are freer, more suggestive and volatile get the upper hand. Hence, the wine can be rich, noble, marked, delicate, subtle, tenuous, full-bodied, complex, even fleeting. But more concrete adjectives come to the aid of this freedom of expression. They are those of the perfumes of nature which recall

the exuberant effusion of dark flowers for red wines and the pale tones of small spring blossoms for white wines. Here we can add fresh or dried fruit, sweets (vanilla and aniseed), herbs and leaves (fresh mint, pine, tobacco), the aromas of spices (pepper, cinnamon), the smells of toasting (coffee, chocolate, tea), those of natural aromas (beer, butter, honey). We could go on, following a fascinating, at times difficult lexical itinerary, assembled for the exact identification of a wine, many wines, through the suggestive force of words.

An ancient secret formula... for wine making

They used an exclusive process of wine making, probably conceived in 1364 by two Florentines, Giovanni di Durante and Ruberto di Guido Bernardi. It consisted of adding a small quantity of raisins to newly made wine and letting it ferment once again to obtain a product devoid of impurities.

THE JOURNEY

The Chianti Classico

The regulations state that the 'Chianti Classico' must contain 75-100% of Sangiovese, an auto cthonous ruby red grape which gives strength and aroma and with age, "tends to turn a garnet red, with an aroma of spices and berries having a fine elegant, round, velvety texture". The remaining 25% consists of other red grapes including the traditional Canaiolo (a maximum of 10%), whereas other grapes favoured by vintners are Cabernet Sauvignon and Merlot. Until a few years ago, a typical addition to this wine was a small quantity of Trebbiano and Malvasia, white grapes which are no longer used.

The Chianti Classico has a dry and balanced taste. When it is still fairly young, it generally preserves a fair amount of acidity. As it matures, it gets more mellow and smooth. It has a strong smell of wine, reminiscent of violets, typical of Sangiovese grapes. It is bright ruby-red but loses its sparkle when ageing, taking on elegant garnet tones.

THE ANTINORI FAMILY

iero Antinori does not own a castle or a villa in the Chianti. However, belonging to a noble family, he has inherited one of the most beautiful palaces of Florence. It is one of those buildings with essential outlines, not allowing for any changes or stylistic additions, a palace where symmetry is felt as an interior necessity rather than an architectural concept or a preference. It expresses the need for order and rationality. It goes without saying that Giuliano da Maiano, the architect who designed it, was one of the most elegant interpreters of the Renaissance, one of those geniuses who had begun his career as a very young man. He had probably worked as a craftsman in one of the more sophisticated crafts such as intarsia but changed his profession soon after. In those years, that is, the middle of the Quattrocento, a period of brilliant minds who were writing the new trends in the history of architecture, Giuliano soon absorbed the teaching of Michelozzo and the great theorist Leon Battista Alberti.

One of his first commissions was Palazzo Boni itself. He set to work on it but his patron soon ran out of funds and had to stop the works. Giuliano walked out enraged, leaving the main part of the building unfinished. In 1506, Niccolò Antinori purchased it and had it completed and extended a few years later by another famous Florentine architect, Baccio d'Agnolo, a close collaborator of Giuliano da Sangallo. Around the middle of the Cinquecento, the Palazzo took on its present-day appearance and became one of the reference models of Tuscan civil architecture. From then on, it also became the prestigious residence of this ancient family and the headquarters of the wine producing firm. Ever since then, the history of Palazzo Antinori and its wines are closely intertwined.

Eight hundred years in wine

Antinoro was the first member in the lineage and Piero is a contemporary member of the family. There is a span of more than eight centuries between them. Eight hundred years of pride in belonging to this family. We met him here, in this palace, situated in the square with their name, also situated at the beginning of Via Tornabuoni, the 'Bond Street' of the most elegant High Society of Florence. It is a building where the intimate Renaissance courtyard is an enchanting model of beauty and the rooms on the 'piano nobile', where the Marchese lives, seem to reflect the atmosphere of Florence during the rule of Lorenzo Il Magnifico.

We leave together for his large wine producing estate towards a friendly part of the Chianti, a countryside in the municipality of San Casciano which is united to the Val di Pesa where it ends. It is a part of the Florentine Chianti where the vineyards and olive groves of the Antinori expand on gentle slopes which begin to rise sharply as soon as we approach Badia a Passignano. The monastery is one of the great spiritual centres of the territory and is still controlled by Vallombrosan monks in whose cellars, 2000 French oak barriques are visible. Here they produce one of the most recent Antinori wines, the *Chianti Classico Badia a Passignano*. "This is our latest jewel" the Marchese tells us proudly "50 hectares of vineyards, almost entirely cultivated with

Sangiovese and a wine, left to mature in these splendid vaulted cellars, ideal for ageing, as they maintain a steady temperature all the year round." We return by car to pay a brief visit to the other farms which have given their name to as many Chianti wines. We stop at a small group of buildings surrounded by a gently sloping vineyard and by the fertile land of Galestro. This is Pèppoli, a farm the Antinori purchased in 1985, to celebrate 600 years of wine production. *Pèppoli* is also an appreciated Chianti Classico. This wine consists of 90% Sangiovese, the protagonist, and 10% Merlot which sweetens the character. This type of wine is still undergoing changes and, with time, it will certainly achieve better results. Our curiosity as wine lovers, encourages us to visit the vineyards of one of the greatest wines in the world, one of those wines which confirms the image of a great producer, extending its lifetime. Obviously we are referring to *Tignanello*. When it was presented at the end of the sixties, some thought it was an oddity for the Chianti but its example was followed by many others. It was the first wine in the Chianti which did not contain white grapes and the first which was left to mature in small oak barrels. It was one of the first wines to contain not only the autocthonous Sangiovese but also the allogenous Cabernet Sauvignon. On the estate of Tignanello, 47 hectares of vineyards are dedicated to this historical wine which is produced only in the best vintages because *Tignanello* must always live up to its reputation. Back to Florence, our journey to the Chianti of the Antinori is now at an end. Tomorrow we could set out on another excursion to the numerous farms that this family of wine growers own in various parts of Italy.

The trade of the Vintner

was a minor Art

With the birth of the

Commune, a flourishing wine

business was developed.

Many Florentine families

were trading in wine and

towards the middle of the

13th century, the Guild

of Vintners was founded,

the most important of the

Guilds. Some of the most

ancient families belonged to

this Guild, as wine production

was destined to become one

of the most outstanding

activities in Florentine history

and some of these families

continue to deal in the wine

business.

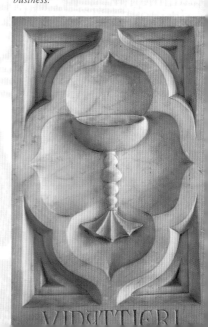

VINATTIERI

A 'SAINT' OF TUSCANY

t is a rich, popular and noble wine. It is rustic, refined, mild and full-bodied. It is a sweet wine which is now produced all over Tuscany with advanced technology and drunk at the end of the meal to accompany home-made cakes or refined pastries. It is also above all a wine for 'meditation' with its fine, dark amber colour. It generally has a strong, multifaceted bouquet. Vin Santo requires a long, patient preparation. It is not only a Tuscan product. Indeed, there are many other Vin Santos produced in several other limited territories all over Italy. However, the distinguishing feature of Tuscan Vin Santo is that it is a much loved and popular product throughout the region, from Florence to Siena, from Pistoia to Arezzo and Lucca.

There are many theories about the origin of its name. It probably took its name from the grapes that were dried in the period around All Saints Day. One of the explanations, though highly unlikely, is that its name can be traced back to the Council of Florence in 1439 which approved the *Laetentur Coeli*, presumed to have united the Church of the Orient and the Church of Rome. On this occasion a pleasant sweet wine was offered to the metropolitan Bessarione, Bishop of Nicea, which he deeply appreciated, exclaiming *"but this is the wine of Xantos"*. The Archbishop naturally referred to the similarity of the wine to another sweet wine he knew very well, produced in the Greek city of Xantos, now Xanthi. From then on, it seems that that delicious wine was renamed Vin Santo.

Until a few decades ago, both in humble peasant homes and the rich cellars of the wealthy, Vin Santo had always been present for a toast. Whenever there was an event to celebrate, the wine made its golden appearance to celebrate any event as a symbol of hospitality and good fortune. Nowadays, its

consumption has partly been reduced but its quality has been considerably improved and now, the more enlightened producers have put on the market a first class wine which is not inferior to other sweet wines anywhere in the world. Vin Santo can vary considerably in colour and this is due to the fact that not everybody produces it with the same grapes. The grapes used are usually Trebbiano and Malvasia, Canaiolo bianco and San Colombano, although some producers add small quantities of other grapes, such as Chardonnay, Grechetto and Pinot. According to Tuscan tradition, the grapes are left to dry on reed mats in a closed, well ventilated room and not directly on the plant as is done with other grapes of the same kind. The maturing is carried out in oak casks where the wine is left for a few years, even if some producers are trying to change the ancient tradition of using chestnut and oak casks.

If a dry wine or demi-sec is desired, it should be made in January, whereas for a sweeter wine it has to be made in February or March. The small barrels are placed in the so-called 'vinsantaie', that is in cellars, generally underground, where there are less variations in temperature. After a minimum of three years, but even four or five, the Vin Santo will be ready with its 16°-17.5°, to heat the souls of so many wine lovers and cultured wine experts. And the Vin Santo of the Chianti Classico, needless to say, is one of the best products in Tuscany. There are at least five varieties: the Sweet and the Dry, with their respective vintages and its 'speciality', Occhio di Pernice. The first four types are made with Trebbiano and Malvasia grapes. They reach 16° and, in the vintage version, are left to mature for four years. Occhio di Pernice has the peculiarity of combining the two traditional grapes with Sangiovese. The end product is a sweet, pleasing and unusual wine.

 f the imagination of a child could come up with the idea of an ancient medieval castle, it would probably be something similar to the small fortification that stands in the Chianti hills close to Florence, set between San Casciano and Greve.

The drawbridge is missing, and there are no knights in their heavy armour, but the rest corresponds perfectly. There are the four beautiful, angular towers, with their perfectly balanced proportions, stressed by a rhythm of flat-topped merlons, and an evocative atmosphere. The paradigm of the Middle Ages, not at all sinister and dark but alert and proud. A complex that links its own fame to a controversial figure from Fiorentine history, a certain Pier Soderini, that was owner of the castle and owes his fame to the fact that he was elected Gonfalonier (Governing magistrate) of the Florentine Republic from 1502 to 1512, in a political period that was very troublesome for the town of Giglio, straddled between the banishment of the Medici family and its successive return. In short, he was a local ruler with very poor political intuition and was not particularly able in the management of public life, but had the important merit of honesty.

But in the Soderini age, the castle had already become a private residence and had left behind its original role of a defence fortification situated on the crucial lines of communication between Florence and Siena.

A complex developed around a medieval tower that in the XIII century found its wine growing and producing vocation.

Ivano Reali, administrator of Beringer Blass Italy, recent owner of the castle, introduces himself to us at the visit. Shortly afterwards we are joined by Silvia Bottelli, the PR consultant. The medieval wine cellars are crammed with casks and oak barrels for ageing. Amongst these walls, solid like rock, there still lingers an ancient soul. A soul that evokes an invisible past that has not disappeared. Coming back into the light of day we see that the castle is similar to a beautiful theatre that is still closed to the spectators. Amongst the new owner's plans is the intention to make it useable, in fact to make it become the heart around which to produce the new Gabbiano spectacle, in the centre of Chianti Classico.

My almost obsessive passion for sounds immediately arouses the desire to see a summer music season, held in the beautiful garden, which has a privileged view over the hills and vines. But then I consider theatrical plays, evocative shows with banquets full of ladies and gentlemen where the wine from here is served. I stop imagining these scenes when we enter the restaurant named Il Cavaliere.

The culinary dishes are prepared by Marco Stabile, a young chef that learned the tricks of the trade at a well-reputed school that belongs to another chef, an old friend of mine and appreciated master of cuisine. This is a young chef that already has the countenance of the great master and announces a personal menu on the lines of a Tuscan tradition lightened and re-appraised by intelligence.

I catch sight of a small flowerbed stuffed with herbs and he immediately notices my interest and picks a bunch of perfumed herbs which then go on to improve and exalt my personalised dishes. His is a rare type of kindness. Failing to disappoint me is the passage of wines which nowadays is defined as a wine tasting session. Without hesitation I commit myself to the reds.

I taste a good *Chianti Classico riserva castello di Gabbiano* in which the recently awakened Sangiovese seems to be still a little riotous in immediately giving its best. I re-try it a few minutes and a patient oxygenation later and find dry and moderately tannic scents with an aftertaste of fruits of the forest that is the true sign of every great Chianti Classico. Decent and worthwhile is *Bellezza*, a Sangiovese IGT (typical to the geographical area) in which there is a clear scent of barrel (now customary to many wines that we taste) that quickly reaches the nose.

Also very interesting is *Alleanza*, another IGT wine but with a completely different nature. This was born from a friendship, (and perhaps even a bet) between two oenologists, Giancarlo Roman, that meticulously follows Gabbiano, and Ed Sbragia, that is involved with the American Beringer Blass enterprises. The two have created a wine by adapting and experimenting and have come up with a very pleasant organic result. This full-bodied red contains 50% Sangiovese, 40% Merlot and 10% Cabernet Sauvignon.

It is an absolute must!

The barrel ageing cellar

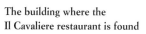

The building where the
Il Cavaliere restaurant is found

THE CHIANTI OF FONTERUTOLI

 n this 16th December 1398, 3 florins 26 soldi, 8 denari to be paid to Piero Tino Riccio for 6 barrels of Chianti wine... we pay the above with a letter from Ser Lapo Mazzei". At the end of the 14th century, a certain esteemed and influential Ser Lapo Mazzei, Notary of the Florentine Signoria, a skilful businessman and great expert of wines, bought Chianti wine. Then his niece, Madonna Smeralda married Piero di Agnolo da Fonterutoli, bringing to her family the property of her spouse. From that moment on, as destiny would have it, the Mazzei, already wine producers for centuries in Carmignano, their birthplace, were no longer obliged to buy Chianti wine. Four centuries later, another Mazzei, Filippo, a restless youth attracted by the spirit of adventure and the love for freedom, triggered off by the ideas of the Enlightenment, was born in this borgo in the second half of the 18th century. Filippo was invited by his friend, Thomas Jefferson, to Monticello in Virginia to plant a vineyard near the residence of the future President of the United States. He went there with a group of excellent Chianti vintners and planted not only this vineyard, but also others and met with great popularity. However, Filippo was also a restless intellectual and deep down he harboured ideas of social justice. Together with Jefferson, he had the time to take part in the American War of Independence and was considered an American patriot by future generations, a patriot who even took part in the drafting of the American Constitution. Thus, an Italian from the Chianti brought the wine culture to the New World and the revolutionary ideas of the Old World. After all this time, there are still members of the Mazzei family in Fonterutoli, the ancient *Fons Rutolae*, which was a resting place for travellers even before 1000 and became a Florentine castle in the long struggles between Florence and Siena. In the borgo situated near Castellina in Chianti, the family carries out an entrepreneurial activity, supported by a deep pride in being the depositaries of important memories of the history of Florence and the Chianti. Outside the beautiful 16th century villa, built on the ruins of a castle, is a lovely Italian garden which slopes gently towards the boundaries of the ancient walls. From here, one can have a truly uplifting view of the Chianti. Outside the property, lies the small borgo with its little country church, stone houses and kind, thrifty people attending to their daily tasks. The Mazzei live in Florence with five children and several grandchildren to give joy to Marchese Lapo and his wife Carla. Filippo and Francesco, the directors of the firm, are at home in Fonterutoli and one can imagine that whenever this great family feels the need to be together, they choose to do so inside the ancient stone buildings of this borgo in the Chianti with its memories.

Let us drink a toast to Fonterutoli

Lapo Mazzei was one of the first to believe in the immense potentialities of Sangiovese. This is testified by the most famous labels produced on his estates, beginning with Siepi, *that was born from a prestigious union of Merlot and Sangiovese. A concentrated wine with sweet tannins that leaves behind an absolute sophistication. We also liked the* Chianti Classico Castello di Fonterutoli, *which can be considered the 'pièce par excellence' of the firm. In this wine, the predominant taste of Sangiovese is combined with a small but decisive presence of Cabernet Sauvignon, the aristocratic grapes to which even a convinced supporter of the red Tuscan grapes like himself, has surrendered, conscious of the successful result of the marriage between these two red grapes, though in very different proportions.*

Casa Mazzei

Marchese Lapo Mazzei gave us this proud, deeply felt message:

"I should like to think that our family tree is like a strong, abundant vine because the entire history of the Mazzei family is continuously connected to vines, cellars and wine"

THE LADY OF VOLPAIA

ou reach the entrance after walking along a side street which is perfectly accessible. It winds through a part of the countryside that still preserves its natural beauty, an area of the Chianti close to Radda where you can imagine the past, when an old peasant with a wrinkled sunburnt face, stops our car with his cart, drawn by a horse as old and weary as himself. He doesn't take any notice of us and continues on his way and, after crossing a little bridge, he draws to one side to let us pass. He looks askance at us and takes off his straw hat to greet us with a deferential gesture which probably hides a note of provocation. It is a gesture of other times. The road begins to climb. On the sides, we can see flourishing rows of vines. When looking up, we understand that the Chianti of wine needs large spaces and we see abundant bunches of grapes pulling down the vines and realize that in a few days' time, they will be harvested by the villagers who will celebrate the birth of a new wine and the renewal of life. Then we reach a circle of ancient walls where we have to stop the car. We are in the circular urban beauty of a castle which has left the echoes of devastating sieges behind it and has started to survive on agriculture. There are still medieval buildings, houses with beautiful late Renaissance doorways. But the large castle-keep and the emblem of Sant'Eufrosino, with its magnificent stone façade revealing the elements of Florentine Renaissance architecture culminating in a slender tympanum which blends with the broken tympanum of the doorway, are the main actors of this impressive stone alley.

Giovannella Stianti Mascheroni, owner of the wine- producing firm and of many buildings in the borgo, introduces us to the secrets of her wines. "Volpaia" she tells us "is a firm I am proud of. It is a modern and highly active firm but succeeds in being unobtrusive". We did our best to hide the productive sector so as to concentrate on the beauty of this small medieval centre. Indeed, the entire borgo is involved in the wine and olive oil production as the vat-rooms, cellars, 'vinsantaia', bottling machinery, store-rooms for oil jars and the presses, though very modern, are kept in the basements, in the buildings, deconsacrated churches and in the buildings of the borgo, united to one another by a surprising underground 'wine duct'." Our hostess invites us into the towering castle-keep to sample her wines. She offers us a little something to eat, to better appreciate the wine and then the cork is unscrewed forever from the bottle of *Castello di Volpaia Riserva,* a

Art in the Castle

For many years, the castle of Volpaia was the centre of one of the most intelligent initiatives dedicated to contemporary art. Young, talented artists exhibited their paintings and sculptures every year during the harvesting. Then unfortunately, Luciano Pistoi, the artistic director of the exhibition died and it was closed down but the vocation to promote artistic works is very strong at the castle. This is why a new festival has been recently founded, this time in the field of music, la Volpaia Jazz Season, with Lucia Minetti as artistic director and with the generous consent of Giovannella Stianti and her husband, Carlo Mascheroni

red wine with an intense fragrance consisting entirely of Sangiovese. The wine has to be swished round in the wine glass to express its qualities in such a brief time and does so soon after. We sip it, but first of all we inhale its fragrance and a still musty, but marked flavour of berries goes up our nostrils. Soon after we can taste a full-bodied, persistent flavour, enhanced by a tannic after-taste which vanishes immediately. It is an excellent wine but meanwhile, another bottle is presented for us to express our inadequate opinion. It is a label which Volpaia is understandably proud of: *Balifico*. In this case, our hostess does not allow us to taste it at once. "This is a subtle wine which requires a long period of airing to give the best of itself – she says handing us the bottle with the precious wine – you have to open it a few hours before a dinner of red meat or game. You will see that the combination is perfect". We return by car and soon after we are back in the midst of the luxuriant vineyards of Volpaia, in that part of the Chianti where the vegetation does not consist only of vineyards and olive groves.

COLLE BERETO,
"SMALL VINEYARD BIG WINE"

olle Bereto, literally means Bereto Hill, and sure enough, the vineyard stands on a hill! A small elevation where a farming factory rises. But it such a sweet hill that it almost loses its geological definition, interposed between pleasant and quick growing vegetation. A run-up of paths, an unexpected cross of trees that enlivens the view, the eccentric rows of the vineyard, the sunnier olive grove behind the house, then the pointed outline of some cypress trees. A silent and hard-working Chianti. A paradigm of what it is and should be like. A house that is as beautiful as it is authentically restored. A house which in the eleventh century was donated by a land-owner of the Radda area to the Church of San Lorenzo a Coltibuono.

The caretaker of these remote stones is a young technician who takes care of the cellars and the vines, and here amongst the stone walls and scents of must and fresh grass, he has found the perfect place for his personal serenity.

Bernardo Bianchi talks to us about the choices made by this small and highly-regarded winery. Choices suggested by a great oenologist, supported by the passionate owners and followed daily by Bernardo's diligence. But we will come back to that later. First there is a story that needs telling.

The story of two lovers that during and cycle from Florence into a Chianti which is very different from that of today.

They were Lorenzo and Franca Pinzauti that were to grow up and go against all advice against mixing business and pleasure, and they joined together not only in matrimony but in work.

They began a business in the fashion sector that over time has grown to such an extent to allow those two lovers that pedaled with their dreams, to return to the Chianti but this time with an eye to buy. And so in 1980 they found their niche in a vineyard, a farmhouse and a nice piece of land that today is Colle Bereto, with 50 hectares of land, on 10 of which there are vines that produce a wine of a medium-high quality.

Bernardo leads us through the vineyard and we taste the entire range of wines. The robust and intense Chianti Classico riserva, in which I seem to get a hint of fruits of the forest, especially blackberries. Immediately after opening, is it slightly held back, but a light and whirling turn around your glass is enough to bring it almost immediately to its best. A few seconds later, the fruity aroma is joined by a scent of toasted coffee which dries and exalts the palate and the taste buds. Completely different are their two IGT wines.

The choice was to use red berries that are not from the area. It was a decision that has paid off. The wines are registered under the following names: *Tocco* and *Cenno* di Colle Bereto.

These names instantly give an archaic air which reminds us of the fact that the Italian language was born here in Tuscany. I indulge on the Tocco (90% Merlot, 10% Sangiovese). On its first contact with the air, this red already has a complex aroma and important structure, and after a few minutes it exhibits a personality that is harmonic and sound, soft and slightly winy, typical of the majority of Merlot wines. What's more difficult, perhaps more risky, is the experiment with Cenno, especially for its possibilities of growth. It is a full-bodied red made with the heretical Pinot Nero; that is, the main grape of the great wines from the Piedmont region of Italy. We have already said that the owners launched an entrepreneurial business in the world of fashion, more specifically in accessories. Their natural flair for design and the importance of image can be seen on the bottles of these two Bordeaux wines.

The labels that are set into the glass, have two beautiful metal seals that show the wine's vintage. It seems to be a completely original idea that aesthetically speaking, is very relevant.

THE HEART OF THE CHIANTI IN FLORENCE

The Colle Bereto vineyard is in the heart of the Chianti, a few hundred metres from Radda.

And Radda has for many years been represented and promoted by a lovely shop that bears its name and sells its produce. But lately the Pinzauti family has had another idea, and that is to bring a little bit of the Chianti countryside into the centre of Florence. And last year they opened a large wine bar with equally large ambitions. At No. Red 5 Piazza Strozzi people can enjoy a bar with a sober and elegant taste, as wine requires.

There are small dishes to try, washed down with the entire range of Colle Bereto wines. In the summer, there are tables outside and you can sit in front of some of the most renowned Renaissance architecture such as Palazzo Strozzi, the palazzo di Benedetto da Maiano, del Cronaca, del Gabinetto Vieusseux and important art exhibitions that the city has managed to organize in recent years.

A GREAT SMALL
WINE GROWER

e was a man of passion, capable of changing his life for a new love and of fighting to the end to defend it. This is not an exaggeration. Sergio Manetti was like this. He had a successful industry, a comfortable but maybe a slightly boring life. Then he discovered that the Chianti was the ideal place for spending week-ends in the countryside, as many do who prefer the expensive whim of having a house to show off rather than to live in. He bought a large farmhouse which had originally been a fortification and planted two vineyards to produce wine for himself and a few friends. He was so successful that after a few years he gave up his industry and plunged into a new activity which still had to be invented. It was the beginning of the seventies.

Today, those two wines have not remained alone even if the Montevertine firm is still small, according to Sergio Manetti, who has always aimed at a very high quality and a family-size business. To understand fully where we have stopped, it is enough to mention the three brands that have made this producer famous. Montevertine, Sodaccio and, above all, Le *Pergole Torte*. These may not mean much to those who are not familiar with wine, but for others, they represent three labels which have long deserved to be at the top of the list of the best Chianti Classico.

Museum of the peasant culture

Sergio Manetti recently passed away, leaving his son Martino with the exciting but difficult task of running this sophisticated wine business and that of directing the small but rare museum of peasant civilization with a collection of tools of former times. It is a private museum which probably deserves to be given more attention by the public Administration.

THE LANDS OF ALBOLA

t the end of the seventies, at the time of the recovery of viticulture in the Chianti, a young Venetian entrepreneur came to this part of the world, a difficult, dignified land like the people who live there. The industrialist looked for a farm to buy, not to show the Tuscans how to make wine but to make a great wine in Tuscany, to upgrade even more the tone of his consolidated activity. He came to Albola near Radda, an ancient borgo, fortified by the Acciaiuoli and felt that the place was ideal to fulfil his 'dream in the Chianti': to make an excellent wine in a suitable setting.

Twenty years have passed since the early beginnings and now Gianni Zonin can say that he has won his challenge also in this field or, better, he has perfectly adjusted the Castello di Albola firm, to the concept of a non-invasive entrepreneurship in keeping with the surroundings: "Each region has its tradition" says Zonin "and each region must have its wine. With this idea in mind, I have tried, in all these years, to produce a Chianti Classico able to express its typical characteristics in the most complete way". Let us take a walk in the borgo, just a short one inside and around the different parts of the buildings, united to one another by the same history and the same stones. As welcomed and warmly received guests,

we felt immediately at home and stopped for lunch when we were able to appreciate the excellent wines produced here. We were offered a full-bodied, powerful red wine, the *Chianti Classico Riserva Castello d'Albola*, a wine matured in small oak barrels which, in our opinion, is a perfect accompaniment to grilled meat dishes. We are then introduced to *Acciaiolo,* a superb Supertuscan wine in which the Sangiovese and Cabernet grapes reduce their differences to form a perfect balance, a truly unforgettable wine.

When saying good-bye, Gianni Zonin invites us to visit the vineyard around the property: "These are the very same vines that produce the grapes used for making *Acciaiolo,* the wine you enjoyed so much". The Villa is surrounded by vineyards cultivated with Sangiovese and Cabernet for making Acciaiolo, thus called to pay homage to the ancient Florentine family, who were the first owners of Albola.

With Gianni Zonin, the number of wines becomes really impressive. His clear ideas, sustained by a passion for the country, a knack for business and also a good deal of courage are the prerogatives of his background as an entrepreneur, not only in terms of numbers but also of quality. Today, Gianni Zonin is the head of a business enterprise with eleven farms in Italy and one in the Unites States.

Zonin

The specialized wine growing estate "Fattoria Castello d'Albola" covers an area of 150 hectares in nine different farms. Naturally, the main cultivation is that of the Sangiovese grape but there are also two traditional grapes, Canaiolo and Malvasia, as well as allogenous ones, Cabernet Sauvignon, Chardonnay and Pinot Nero.

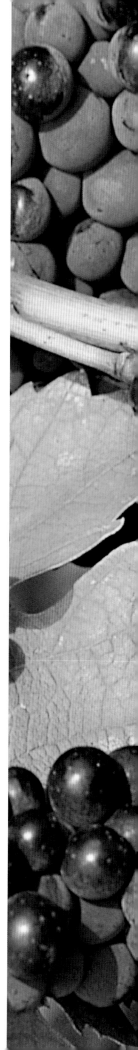

BOCCACCIO'S FLASKS

t seems presumptuous to consider the flask, the typical blown glass container with a full, round belly, lined with straw as an object which should be given a Tuscan DOC (a brand denoting the purity of origin). It has been a sign of festivity on dining tables for centuries. And yet this rustic glass container with its simple, essential form, is typical of Tuscany and even more so, of Florence. Until two or three years ago, the smooth, elegant form of a glass bottle was rarely seen on Tuscan tables. For red wine, of course, there was the fiasco of wine, the natural dwelling, the simple, cheerful container of the grape juice that accompanied the daily meals. To give a brief outline of this container, we have to refer to the artistic iconography which, in similar cases, is of greater help than any other record. In the paintings of 14th century artists we can already see glass bottles similar to flasks. One of the first flasks, thickly lined with straw, is depicted around the middle of the Trecento by Tommaso da Modena in the fresco cycle painted on the

Modena in the fresco cycle painted on the pillars of the Church of San Niccolò in Treviso, relating the stories of St. Jerome and St.Agnes. In one part of the large painting, hung on a nail on a wall, we can see a flask, entirely covered with reeds, as was the custom in those times. The painter came from Emilia and the town was Veneto. Therefore, Tuscany, defeated in this remote iconographic challenge has the upper hand in the field of... literature. Indeed, in his *Decameron*, and more precisely in two of his *Novelle* (VIII, IX day; II, VI day) Boccaccio refers to the flask as the container for 'vermilion wine' and he also informs us about its varying dimensions. We know from Messer Boccaccio that in those times, they used a large flask, called the *quarto* which contained 5.7 litres of liquid, a middling one, the *mezzo quarto* which contained about half the quantity and a small one, called the *metadella* which contained just over 1 litre.

Moreover, we know from documents that the profession of the *fiascaio* (flask maker) already existed at the beginning of the 14th century in the Val d'Elsa. This craftsman was

specialized in the production of these containers. All this is related by Silvia Ciappi in her brief study "Wine and glass: bottles, glasses and flasks in the Middle Ages", included in her more extensive work *From Kantharos to Bordolese, a history of wine containers*, published by the Centro di Studi chiantigiani "Clante" which we believe to be one of the most complete on the subject.

From the 16th century, the flask frequently appears in the paintings of the ancient masters, not only Tuscans, to show its widespread diffusion beyond the boundaries of Tuscany, even if it is more frequent in the paintings of Florentine artists (e.g. the splendid flasks painted in the still lifes of Empoli). But the history of the flask is closely connected to the history of glass and the 'culture of materials', at which point the problem becomes more complicated. Indeed, as many sustain, the glass blowers of the Val d'Elsa, already famous at the beginning of the second millennium for their glass furnaces, were those who probably exported this form of blown glass, together with more sophisticated glasses and other kinds of bottles, to other parts of the peninsula. Whatever the answer, there is no doubt that from a certain period onwards, the flask disappeared from the tradition of other Italian regions. However, in Tuscany it not only survived but also consolidated its presence until our times. This is an unwritten document which cannot be produced as an objective proof but cannot be overlooked.

BROLIO OR THE RICASOLI FIRIDOLFI

The origins of the

Chianti Classico

Baron Francesco Ricasoli Firidolfi now leads the industry of the most glorious label of the Chianti, that ancient Chianti which came into existence with the League including Radda, Gaiole, Castellina and... Brolio has been one of the leading centres in the history of wine which has seduced the world for almost 1000 years.

Bettino Ricasoli is the inventor of the oenological formula of the present-day Chianti:

"Wine draws most of its aroma and some strong sensations from Sangioveto. It takes a certain mildness from Canaiolo which softens the sharpness of the former without reducing the aroma with which it is endowed. Malvasia which should be added in minor proportions to vintage wines, tends to dilute the product of the first two grapes, reducing the flavour".

He is always present, everywhere, the 'Iron Baron', the great statesman of a new Italy. He earned this awe-inspiring nick-name because of his decisive, inflexible character which helped him to have a great political career and to produce his 'new wine' in Brolio, the new wine of the Chianti. The baron was a determined man, obstinate and enthusiastic, a winner. At the age of twenty, he administered the wine

firm and decided to improve the ancient wine, already deeply appreciated, but with an outdated organization. As he was not lacking in self-confidence, he tried out different solutions, blending Cabernet, Pinot, Grenache and Carignano grapes having a rich, full-bodied flavour, which do best in more fertile soil than the dry gravel of this part of the Chianti. He performed these experiments over a long period and the result was that the autocthonous clones of Sangiovese seemed to have a stronger character, more pride and personality. As a proof of this, he wrote to his friend Paolo Studiati: *"... until that day, I had not succeeded in obtaining from the soils of Brolio a wine that could be compared to Sangioveto for aroma, grace and smoothness by adding Pinot, Cabernet, Grenache, Carignan and Alicanter."*

But the Sangiovese needed a bit of warmth to express its talents completely. So the baron thought that another, less structured and less noble grape than the first, one more inclined to adjust easily to tastes, could soften the sturdy Sangiovese. He therefore decided that a small percentage of Canaiolo could instil more softness into the Chianti and that the use of a very small quantity of Malvasia could also be added, even if he was of the opinion that this grape could have been excluded altogether, thus foreseeing one century earlier, the trends of viticulturists today.

The Brolio wine produced by the Barons Ricasoli Firidolfi as far back as the Middle Ages, thanks to the 'Iron Baron', began to write the modern history of the Chianti Classico, becoming one of the most prestigious wines of the territory. In the last decades, the leadership of this estate was in the hands of another Bettino, the great grandson of the illustrious forefather. For some time now, this leadership has been handed on to Bettino's son Francesco, the 32nd baron of Brolio. Thanks to his determined and courageous decisions, he has managed to recover the prestige of this wine following a period of a difficult reorganization of the firm.

Hence, Chianti Classico above all, but not only. In Brolio, as in many other estates of the Chianti, there is a trend to diversify the production. Indeed, besides the almost incomparable *Chianti Classico Castello di Brolio,* by now almost a pure Sangiovese, *Casalferro,* a brand defined as a 'laboratory-wine' has met with great favour, just because "it is trying to enhance the properties of Sangiovese combined with the grapes of a similar category such as Cabernet Sauvignon and Merlot." These grapes are added in different quantities at each harvest, according to the chemical results obtained.

"The property of Brolio belongs to the Communes of Gaiole in Chianti and, to a lesser degree, to Castelnuovo Berardenga and covers an area of more than 1200 hectares, mainly with oak and chestnut forests, whereas firs and larches prevail on the hills. 26 hectares are cultivated with olive groves and 227 with vineyards, with considerable variations in the height and typology of the territory".

A 'THINKING' CELLAR

ine is strange, strange because it is capable of arousing lasting passions in time. This is a brief history of the passion of a German entrepreneur who, some years ago, built a cellar in the heart of the historical Chianti, near Castello di Brolio, called the Colombaio di Cencio. Unlike many others he did not want to buy an old farm, restore it and dedicate it to wine production. Werner Wilhelm went further, he had a cellar built with all the characteristics and materials typical of the Chianti, a modern interpretation of an ancient rural building. He planned a cellar for the future, endowed with a complex computerized system of heating, cooling and running the entire wine making process. Besides this, also the most advanced plants for pressing and filtering have been foreseen as well as *barrique* vats which are continually renewed. The aim of all this is to produce an outstanding wine. The methods soon bore fruit, if we consider that the activity was begun only in 1998 and international appreciation was not slow to come. We are accompanied by Jacopo Morganti, a pure Chiantigiano and director of this 'thinking' cellar. We tasted together with him the only two brands now in production, *I Massi del Colombaio*, a Chianti Classico Riserva, and *Futuro*, a Supertuscan which is achieving great results only now as it is a complex wine with an outstanding structure which emanates a very delicate bouquet where we can clearly distinguish the fragrance of cherry and vanilla. We felt very enthusiastic about this wine when tasting it. It seemed to issue fruity tones, absolutely harmonious with one another and even an after taste, reminiscent of chocolate. A wine for ageing which will no doubt improve with time.

A vineyard of the future

In the text, we referred to the efficient management and courage of Baron Giovanni Ricasoli Firidolfi. The following case is one of these exceptional examples.

In Cacchiano, 7 hectares of land were planted with 6589 vines.

A new type of tree-wine was planted for this wine estate.

"Till the present time, the Castello di Cacchiano is the only example in the Chianti Classico of a farm that has gone beyond the limits of the accepted agronomical pratice in vineyards, achieving the highest density of plants per hectare ever reached till now".

THE RICASOLI OF CACCHIANO

It is a noble country residence which openly declares its fortified origins. This is how we see Cacchiano when we get there as guests of the young owner, Giovanni Ricasoli Firidolfi, the president of the Foundation and the League of the Chianti and the last but one generation (as he has a small son) of a branch of the famous family. The Baron spends his life partly in the family palace in Via Maggio, Florence and partly inside of this splendid fortification which was built more than 1000 years ago on the hills of Monti in Chianti. This is a crucial point where the Florentines and the Sienese fought each other in battle for long periods and where wine has always been the undisputed protagonist of the agricultural economy. But the wine growers of Cacchiano carried out the activity with entrepreneurial concepts only in 1974. It was Baron Alberto and his spouse, Elisabetta Balbi Valier, who created the first label, the *Chianti Classico Castello di Cacchiano*. The management of the estate has now been handed on to their son, Giovanni, who has made important investments in the vineyards and in the cellars. In a property which stretches for about 200 hectares, 31 cultivated with vineyards and 35 with olive groves, this young entrepreneur is aiming at the maximum improvement of his production. But let us ask him to tell the story: "I'm convinced that the high quality of the end product should be the result of careful work on the vines and of a correct interpretation of the *terroir* which distinguishes one area from another and defines the characteristics of individual vintages. We are trying to obtain an increasingly more typical, recognizable wine."

We visit the cellars for making and maturing wine, cellars which have recently been renewed and we stop for a toast with a couple of bottles which draw our attention as curious wine lovers. The Baron himself acts as host and offers us a *grand cru* where he has skilfully uncorked the right quantity for a sampling of *Chianti Classico Castello di Cacchiano*. It is a wine where the harsh and tannic taste of Sangiovese is mellowed with other grapes among which we seem to recognize the vinous, fruity fragrance of Merlot. We ask him which ones they are, as we cannot smell the unmistakable aristocratic but somewhat conditioning touch of Cabernet Sauvignon. "90% Sangiovese, 5% Merlot, 5% Canaiolo, black Malvasia and Colorino" is the answer. With an inviting smile, Giovanni Ricasoli offers us another glass of wine to taste. It is a rich wine with a persistent and complex bouquet. It is a wine with an eccentric personality but in this case too we can observe the absence of Cabernet. We ask him if it only contains Sangiovese. This time, we are not happy with it. "90% Sangiovese, 10% Canaiolo, black Malvasia and Corodino, a very Tuscan wine of the new generation", answers the Baron. The *Millennium* is, no doubt, the most aristocratic label of the firm.

Maybe it is just because of this courageous choice of not including Cabernet in his wines and focusing mainly on a maximum improvement obtained from traditional grapes that the work carried out until now by Giovanni Ricasoli has already been appreciated by experts as one of the most interesting and innovative in the sector of wine production.

SAN FELICE
A BORGO IN THE CHIANTI

an Felice is delicately balanced between simplicity and abundance. The entrance is sober, essential, Tuscan, without gates or doors with the friendly but frugal and unassuming welcome, typical of an ancient agricultural borgo which has not renounced to its quiet everyday life. The hospitality offered is generous, rich and elegant. It welcomes you in the form of the refined setting of a restaurant lit externally by a low, diffused light which creates a natural, relaxing reflection. This atmosphere is very much alive near the swimming pool which blends so well with the ancient surrounding stone buildings and the refined interior decoration of the suites and rooms of the Relais. We are on an estate, but we have not yet felt the typical bustle of business activity. As in a perfectly organized microcosm, everything flows without your realizing it. All this goes to the benefit of those who choose San Felice to spend a few days of unusual, stimulating serenity.

Giovanni Gorio, an engineer from Milan, chose the countryside of the Chianti closer to Siena in which to live and work. He controls this composite productive centre with the skill of a director who knows he can rely on a good script and a successful setting. He is a director who prefers to stay behind the scenes to lead the dance without losing control of everything that is going on only intervening if an interpreter needs advice to act his part better. He himself takes us around to appreciate all the secrets of San Felice. The first 'secret' is the revelation of the borgo. It consists of a group of stone houses, which show again their ancient, simple dignity thanks to an architectural rehabilitation which correctly observes the traditional canons of the Chianti. The different parts of the buildings belong to different periods even if the unaccustomed eye would be deceived because everything is built in stone and everything seems to belong stylistically to the same period. The main palace and other buildings were built in the 19th century but behind the large square of access is concealed the small medieval borgo which has generally maintained its original characteristics. On the subject we can read: "The loggias, covered spaces, external stairways, dovecots, little roads that lead to small squares, the paving in cotto and stone and the sheds (barns isolated for fear of fires) are all typical elements of the medieval borgo in the Chianti".

We came here, above all, for the wine of San Felice which is the force of attraction of the borgo. At lunch, Gorio uncorks a bottle of *Vigorello*. We begin with a historical label created here, in this very place, just when there was the need to try out something new. Agreed, tradition should be observed and particularly

173

The exquisite wine of San Felice

In a letter dated 11th December 1683, addressed to Lelio del Taja, then proprietor of San Felice, one reads: "To better please the taste of those Signori, I tried to find a good wine and to tell them that it came from these parts, for they have always expressed great interest as they give more importance to a flask of wine from this place than anything else".

appreciated but now and then, a few exceptions to the rule give us the idea of open-mindedness, a sign of mental curiosity and intelligence.

What I mean is that this wine gave rise to a great deal of controversy when it was presented at the end of the sixties. It was an experiment which included the combination with 'heretical' grapes. It was not a Chianti Classico but a Chianti with the addition of Cabernet Sauvignon, a grape that many others have tried out in recent years and which is now, though to a lesser degree, normally added to the grapes of the Chianti Classico.

In these years, the first big investments in the territory for the revival of wine production were made. In 1978, in this atmosphere of renewal, the Riunione Adriatica di Sicurtà R.A.S. purchased San Felice whose vineyards now cover more than 200 hectares. This area is not only dedicated to wine production but also includes a space for serious experimentation carried out together with the Universities of Florence, Siena and Pisa. Naturally these experiments deal with viticulture and especially with the selection of clones, the preservation of the genetic heredity of each type of grape and the most advanced forms of cultivating them.

We have spoken about the wines of San Felice and now we want to talk about the oil of San Felice. We were able to taste it during lunch. It was somewhat pungent, very agreeable, slightly fruity with a strong taste. It is an unusually balanced oil, the product of accurate work, carried out on 150 hectares cultivated with olive groves. Numerous olive trees surround this relais in the countryside to protect it from the bedlam of present-day life.

ANTONIO FALLINI IN SAN FELICE

he profession of a chef is by now, and probably just so, identified with the cultured and creative image of an artist and researcher. The traditional figure of a good chef has long since come to an end: a well-built physique, a merry personality, a great spirit of abnegation around the stove and traditional dishes which have become unimaginative but consolidated by time and repetition. Nowadays a leading or renowned chef puts great emphasis on his public image; an image which is exceptionally well-groomed and obviously free from an expanding waistline.

In the kitchen the chef has a large group of helpers that are always perfectly organised and move in unison to his commands. He is a maitre de cuisine or a master of the kitchen that rarely intervenes during the cooking stage, but prefers to oversee the others working. In short, he is a soloist, one that, at the ritual, (and in a certain sense, sacred) moment of the representation, already has everything organised. He has already tried and re-tried the dishes, almost always little works of art that join together aesthetics and taste, that he will now go and present to his guests. Antonio Fallini falls into the category of those that interpret the profession with this profound conviction. And the results are absolutely worth the wait. With the anxiety of a man that continually wants to know more, to deepen his knowledge and to experiment, Fallini has spent many years in the world's best restaurants: in the United States, in England and in Japan. And we find him at the top of the best restaurants. Yet when he finds success in one place, he leaves to begin all over in another place, to put himself to the test and experiment with a new reality. He came here to San Felice not very long ago. He returned after a short-lived estrangement for a new bet with himself... "I have returned to stay for a long time, perhaps for ever, who knows?", he confesses.

We experience first hand some of his dishes on a warm evening at the beginning of the summer. We realise that our chef has not renounced the traditional cuisine from the Chianti hills and generally the region of Tuscany; in fact quite the opposite. He has made it his own to such an extent that he has given it a new lease of life, and allowed it to discover new possibilities. In short, he has changed its appearance, given it a few useful finishing touches and reinvigorated it, all without distorting its profound nature. And so when we taste the plate of Ravioli with pigeon in a reduced Chianti Classico sauce, we feel grateful to the sacrifice made by the little bird and by the able hand of a man who has succeed in making the most of the aromas for the pleasure of our taste buds whilst not overpowering us with excessive flavours and overcooking.

Defending a tradition

"The freshness of produce, attention to tradition and a desire to re-experience that tradition. These are the simple rules that Poggio Rosso has always obeyed".
Birgit Fleig, manager of the Relais, underlines the strong Tuscan connotation of the restaurant's cuisine. It is a choice that has been strongly defended by the management of San Felice, even in times, by now belonging to the recent past, when the tendency was to sweep away anything connected with the past, not distinguishing between the grain and the bran, and grain has always played a big part in Tuscany style cuisine.

OIL IN... EARTHENWARE

The olive groves that cover extensive stretches of the region and which seem to be improved by the gentle undulation of the hills in the Florentine and Sienese countryside, are a fairly recent source of wealth. The intense cultivation of olive trees dates back to the second half of the 19th century; as the production of oil had been far more limited in former centuries. At one time, food was seasoned with lard as they could not afford oil which was too expensive and therefore only for the well-to-do or also used in cosmetics. It was only in the 15th century, that they began to export locally produced oil and to realize that most of Tuscany is suited to olive cultivation as the soil is sufficiently dry and well exposed to the sunshine. In an excellent guide of the Gambero Rosso (by the two authors Marco Sabellico and Marco Oreggia, editors of a series of books which are remarkable for the accuracy of information and the attractive appearance) we can read: "Tuscan extra virgin olive oil is green in colour with slight tones of golden yellow; it smells of vegetables, reminiscent of fresh grass and artichokes. It has an intense, rich taste of fruit and vegetables, leaving a hot after-taste of almonds. Among the areas dedicated to oil production, we would also like to mention the Chianti Classico...". The numerous Tuscan extra virgin olive oils, the delicate one of the Lucchesia and the hills around Livorno, the thicker and more tasty ones of the Maremma, the milder, typical kinds of the Florentine, Chianti and Sienese hills are all of a fine quality, although the oil produced in the magic territory between Florence and Siena is considered to have a special, insuperable quality. About a quarter of the over 25 million olive trees present in Tuscany are found in the province of Florence. This is a very important statistic. Moreover, oil has remarkable therapeutic properties. It produces good cholesterol HDL which protects us from arteriosclerosis and cardiovascular diseases and, thanks to the presence of

antioxidants, it defends the organism from ulcers and gastritis. A drop of extra virgin olive oil can also be given to babies. Thanks to a high concentration of linolenic acid, also found in milk, it strengthens and increases the mineral content in the bones favouring the production of nerve cells. A good Tuscan consumes extra virgin olive oil as a food and for seasoning but only in cases of absolute necessity, for frying. We would like to add one last gastronomic observation though it would probably be more exact to speak of advice. The new, recently pressed oil should be added raw to vegetable soups, ribollita or boiled beans whereas more mature oil (several months old) is particularly indicated for seasoning salads, radicchi (wild salads) and pinzimonio (raw vegetables) and for cooking.

The D.O.P. oil of the Chianti Classico
Tuscany is an avant garde region for the norms regulating oil production, norms conceived for improving the quality of the product and for protecting its authenticity. Extra virgin olive oil produced in the Chianti Classico has recently obtained the D.O.P. label (Denominazione d'Origine Protetta, i.e., denomination of protected origin) which like wine, aims at safeguarding and further improving the production of Chianti wine through rigid rules of selection. As in grapes, there are autocthonous olives from which oil is produced. We can read: "The extra virgin olive oil of the *Chianti Classico* is produced with olives from olive groves, registered as D.O.P., with at least 80% from the plants of Frantoio, Correggiolo, Moraiolo, Leccino, individually or blended together and with a maximum of 20% from plants of other varieties in the area".

THE BADIA OF 'GOOD HARVESTS'

The first official history of Chianti wine was written by the Vallombrosan monks inside these walls, no longer the same as those of the ancient abbey. Inside their closed cells, they spent their days in prayer, meditation and writing. But when they went outside, in accordance with the rules of St.Benedetto and the founding father St. Giovanni Gualberto, they dedicated themselves to work in the fields, often continuing their prayers. They were 'specialized' in the cultivation of vines: they had planted the first vines around the abbey at the beginning of the second millennium. This history describes the origins of the place which is undeniably one of the most stirring and typical areas of the Chianti for the beauty of the sacred complex and the natural surroundings. Today it is no longer inhabited by monks and there is a family, the Stucchi Prinetti, who have been the owners and custodians of the splendid abbey and active producers of wines for the past 150 years. In the last four decades in particular, thanks to the dedication of Pietro Stucchi Prinetti and his wife, Lorenza de' Medici, the Chianti Classico of Badia a Coltibuono has been one of the important names that has contributed to the rebirth of the modern Chianti. Today, the estate which does not only live on viticulture but is also a multifaceted structure, is perfectly organized in every way for accommodation and catering.

It is run by their children Roberto, who is the director and an excellent oenologist and Emanuela, who is responsible for the marketing and sales and has recently become the President of the Consortium of Historical Brands. On the 50 hectares, cultivated with vineyards, are produced famous labels such as *Badia a Coltibuono Riserva* and *Badia a Coltibuono Selezione Roberto Stucchi*, a pure Sangiovese which gives excellent results for the rich bouquet and the well-balanced tannins, strong but not excessive, leading to a delightful after taste of berries and irises. During this brief journey through the vineyards we observed that Badia is one of the few wine farms where they had made a choice that was difficult until a few years ago. It is now rewarding those who were against the use of combining French grapes with Sangiovese. Here, this policy has always been pursued because all the wines which claim the right of being called Chianti Classico only contain Sangiovese or the addition of a minimum quantity of Canaiolo, according to tradition.

QUERCIABELLA

uerciabella is almost the emblem of an agricultural borgo in the Chianti. Nevertheless, most of these structures have been constructed recently, even if all of them have been built, rigidly observing the architectural 'philology' of the Chianti: stone façades and roofs with cotto tiles. It belongs to a well-known family of Milanese entrepreneurs, Giuseppe Castiglioni, the father and his son Sebastiano Castiglioni, who came here to the Chianti in 1972. It is an industrial undertaking in the countryside of Greve which has established itself as one of the most outstanding and innovative in the field of wine production. We were invited to taste the wines.

We had heard about the *Batàr*, a Supertuscan wine which is one of the "fortes" of the estate, a Tuscan IGT, consisting of 65% Chardonnay and 35% Pinot bianco, fermented in small barriques. For us too, who have a natural tendency to prefer red wines, the encounter with this white wine with a rich, spicy bouquet, was revealing.

But Chianti Classico is always present. The one we are tasting in Querciabella, an almost pure Sangiovese with a low addition of Merlot, Cabernet Sauvignon and Syrah, presents a fine structure, markedly tannic, vaguely reminiscent of irises.

Dievole

The Dievole property is made up of approximately 400 acres of which 96 are dedicated to specialized vines. The wine cellar which winds along two corridors reaching a length of almost 200 metres, becomes the scene of a great party every harvest time where all of Dievole's residents come to celebrate.

A DAY IN DIEVOLE

By chance I come across a presentation of Dievole and its wines. I read: "Being a farmer involves more than knowing how to dig, hoe and plough the land, how to lop, reap and gather the crops, it means knowing more than anything else, how to mix the lightness of the sky into the land." Goodness! What a bold statement. I'm not used to reading such poetry. It seizes me unexpectedly. It intrigues me yet irritates me a bit too. I simply must meet the author of such a compelling message which is the same person who has brought Dievole back to life, Mario of Dievole, officially known as Mario Felice Schwenn, who, not even forty years old, is a master of communication; someone tells me; a phenomenon of the media, someone else. At this stage my curiosity begins to get the better of me. A great wine which I already know of, enticing voices which allure me and that statement which I must face, which I

must understand. Reasons enough to justify an interesting investigation.

So here I am in Dievole. I have an appointment with this entrepreneur who makes dreams come true. One of his young workers takes me onto his land. A beautiful villa from the late seventeenth century, genuine farmhouses doted around a vast area of vines and woods. In short it is one amongst many of the aesthetically relevant places in the Chianti where they produce an important wine and an oil just as valued. But something noticeably different strikes me as soon as I start down a long Cypress-lined avenue. A country-side which cannot be said to be organised, yet neither is it untidy, strikes you with its farmhouses which are not like those we see in shiny magazines, but farmhouses in the true sense of the word.

Houses which have been restored carefully, whose soul still shines through. Before reaching the villa I come across a remote outline of a church-oratory which has been there since the fifteenth century, even though it seems to be from much more recent times. Junior Appiani, my guide, welcomes me inside the building and his face takes on an ecstatic expression, like someone who is about to come into contact with something sacred. He takes a little leather bag: "It's the first time that I have actually held it in my hands. Mario told me to show you what it holds", he said. He took out six coins, minted in Lucca for a long time until

1080 and which, 10 years later on 10th May 1090, were paid to the manager of the Carthusian monastry in Piescola, by a group of farmers, with the addition of two capons and three loaves of bread in order to be able to rent and work the land in Dievole. Small circles of silver which over a thousand years ago sanctioned the beginning of the farming life of this place. And which now, perfectly reproduced, mark, like a sign of nobility, the Bordeaux of wine of the highest prestige in the vineyard, the Novecento, a Reserve Chianti Classico which expressed the best reasons of the Sangiovese Ora. Then we progress onto the wine-cellar, followed by a tasting rest in the courtyard. That evening we dine with Edmund J. Diesler, friend, oenologist and close partner of Mario Schwenn. Diesler tells me in much detail about the specific activity of the vineyard. He appears to be a satisfied man. I ask him if it is so. He looks at me a little oddly, then breaks into a huge smile. "Well, working here with Mario is a special thing". The meeting with Mario didn't take place because something came up. But his way of running this company is immediately visible. Social conventions are not respected, what I mean is that rigid roles do not exist and neither does a rigid organisation. There are human beings who exist here just to work with enthusiasm. It is as though everyone had the sensation of being an important link in this management with the philosophy of a smile and the art of welcoming people. The enthusiasm of an enlarged family which works without suffering social differences, and without a boss in the true sense of the word.

The masters of the vines

The Dievole wines make a mark on tradition, that is the protradition.
Let me explain. Many of the wine businesses in the Chianti are trying to value the autochthonous clones of the Chianti, but that is an exaggeration! Okay so Sangiovese is fine and for many it is a trademark, and excellent for the Canaiolo, which for the main part is now overlooked, welcome the Colorino that very few vineyards consider. But when you discover that in the sixteen vines of the vineyard the population founders of the Tuscan wine archaeology are preserved, a species in extinction but that isn't dying out completely thanks to the choice of this wine company, the thing makes you marvel. And what satisfaction! ...the origins of our wine industry history with the soul of a studious type who discovered the remains of a dead city or the paintings of an ancient master: Ancellotta, Barsaglina,

Foglia Tonda, Aleatico, Ciliegiolo, Prugnolo Gentile, Mammolo, Seragiolo. And other than all these, witnesses of a more recent history, which here is defined as classic contemporaries such as Canaiolo a Raspo Rosso, the Malvasia Nera and various clones of the Sangiovese.

The work is carried out by wine masters, even in this case the definition coined is suggestive and tense with respect to an industry: cultivation. Others would define such protagonists of the countryside as simple farmers, here they are paid the honour that they deserve. I catch a glimpse of Armando at work. He points out Junior to me. Others are working in vines further away. Their faces appear on the label on one of the most interesting wines of the vineyard, Il Rinascimento, 80% Malvasia Nera, 20% Colorino, a wine which is made the old fashioned Tuscan way. It is a wine which allows "all of its varying character" to shine through, writes the same Mario. "A wine which confiscates the vigour, which takes on the perfumes of the yield in an olfactory range which has never been seen before".

Armando, as I was saying, I don't know what the other masters of vineyards are called, but in their faces they all have the DNA of Duccio and Simone Martini. The DNA of Dievole and Siena. To understand the reason why those proud words about mixing the land with the sky were spoken, becomes very easy to understand at the end of this visit. Dievole is tactile and full of emotion, it is both feminine and virtuous. It is the clone of a patriarchal family where all are equal before the land that brought them into the world and gives them to live off. Because Dievole is like an old book which you flick through for the first like having the feeling that you are part of it.

CONSORTIUM OF
HISTORICAL BRANDS
CHIANTI CLASSICO

those who want to get to know Niccolò Machiavelli, the famous writer and politician who left an immortal mark of his fine intellect in many of his works, only have to stop among these ancient houses of Sant'Andrea in Percussina and imagine this personality. Machiavelli lived here during an unfortunate period of his life. In a famous letter to his friend Francesco Vettori, he himself wrote on the 10th of December 1513 about his stay here: *"Together with these [that is with the customers of an inn] I spend all day, playing 'cricca', 'trich-trach' which leads to innumerable quarrels and endless attacks with insulting words and most of the time we bet a coin and they can hear us shouting even in San Casciano"*. The playful and somewhat vulgar side of this great intellectual comes as a pleasant surprise. He continues: *"At sunset I return home and enter my studio; and at the entrance I take off my peasant's clothing, full of mud and mire and put on my royal, courtly attire; and decently dressed, I enter the ancient courts of ancient men..."*. The house where Machiavelli lived in that period should correspond to the present Villa Bossi-Pucci, well-known as 'l'Albergaccio'; whereas the inn where he rowdily spent his free time is probably a shop-cellar where you can taste local specialities accompanied with excellent wine. Just in front of the inn are the headquarters of the Consorzio del Marchio Storico – Chianti Classico, the organization responsible for the diffusion, improvement and control of this great wine.

Consorzio del Marchio Storico - Chianti Classico

"In order to protect the production of the Chianti Classico, a group of 33 producers met in Radda on 14th May 1924 to found the Consortium for the Protection of Chianti wine and its original brand. Ever since, this organization, later known as the Consorzio del Marchio Storico – Chianti Classico, deals with guaranteeing its quality and promotion." Now the number of its members has increased enormously and exceeds 600 members (250 of whom produce wine with their own label) and represent more than 80% of the general production of the Chianti Classico with their 5000 hectares registered in the Albo dei Vigneti. In 1996, the Chianti Classico became an independent D.O.C.G. With a ministerial decree of 5th August 1996, a separate set of rules was created for the denomination of the 'Chianti Classico'.

Text supplied by Consorzio del Marchio Storico

The tasks of the Consortium

The internal organization of the Consortium provides the structures necessary for carrying out the institutional tasks that concern the qualification of the product, controls of the production, the promotion of the brands and the wines of its members. The technical bureau of the Consortium imposes strict controls on its members. Indeed, the latter must observe the indications of the technicians of the Consortium and submit their products for the organoleptic evaluation of the tasting board and the most rigid chemical analyses in compliance with the law. For instance, every year, after the bottling of the wine, the 'standard of the vintage' of the Chianti Classico is established which, thanks to a high number of samples representative of the entire territory, select the average characteristics of the wine produced that year (more than 90 samples are taken): the wine produced by the members is accepted only if its values correspond to the average values of the standard Chianti Classico.

The technical service also carries out research and experiments in the field of agronomy and collaborates with the Consorzio Vino Chianti Classico to implement a project for the present reimplantation of vineyards. The renewal of the Chianti vines is being carried out and establishes the replacement of about 75% of the old vineyards, now at the end of their productive activity. This renewal which will be concluded by 2010-2012 is mainly based on results obtained during recent years of research and experimentation in the field of Progetto Chianti Classico 2000. The experimental project has dealt with different subjects including: the control of the bioagronomical behaviour and oenological value of some already approved clones of the most important black grapes (first of all Sangiovese), research on stocks and cultivation techniques. The research also includes a ten-year programme for the clonal selection of materials already existing on the territory, aiming at discovering the existence of presumed clones for approval. With this in mind, it should be remembered that

With this in mind, it should be remembered that in 1999, 4 clones of Sangiovese selected in the vineyards of the Chianti Classico and hence belonging to our territory, were approved.

The rural District of the Chianti

In the last few years, the Consortii for the protection and improvement of the territory of the Chianti Classico (Chianti Classico, Marchio Storico, Olio D.O.P., Terre del Chianti) have become promotors of initiatives which aim at obtaining the denomination of Distretto rurale (rural District) for the territory itself. The motivations at the basis of this request, came from several considerations which are important for the producers and the local economy in general. Firstly, the economic structure that was created by the wine producing firms of the Chianti Classico has taken on the features of a 'system' or rather, of a district, distinguished by a strong integration of activities connected to one another (viticulture, tourist accomodation, handicrafts, oenogastronomy, etc.) whose intrinsic 'property' consists in the research of the increasingly better 'quality' of services and products supplied. Secondly, the request for the denomination of Distretto emerged from a need to guarantee the sustainability of the economic growth of the sector, as it is only through the adoption of specific policies that economic competitiveness can be increased.

The Foundation for the Protection of the Chianti Classico

The Foundation is a non-profit making body, engaged in the preservation of the artistic and environmental heritage of the territory.

Text supplied by the Consorzio del Marchio Storico

188

The Lega del Chianti is clearly inspired by the institution, fouded at the beginning of the 14th century, when Gaiole, Castellina and Radda united under the standard of a stylized Gallo Nero (black cock) with a military organization but also with a Statute in which the rules to administer the vineyards were established, together with precise indications for the production of wine.

Today, the Lega del Chianti, re-established in 1970, from all parts of the world, intends to give a new boost to life in the countryside and to the religious feeling inspired by friendship and solidarity which is natural to it. It also aims at incentivating numerous initiatives, in other words, everything that this territory, rich in history and art, traditions and the beauty of its natural surroundings, has to offer.

As in ancient times, the League is divided into three parts, the Terzieri: Gaiole, Castellina and Radda, whilst Florence, Siena and Greve form the Pivieri (parishes) with a similar counterpart in Germany, Switzerland and Austria.

The members of this complex organization including an important one, connected to the Church, carry out different roles, all directed at protecting and guiding the future of the Chianti. The themes confronted and debated concern those cherished by this area: painting, architecture, wine, the environment.

Since 1998, Baron Giovanni Ricasoli Firidolfi has been Captain General of the League.

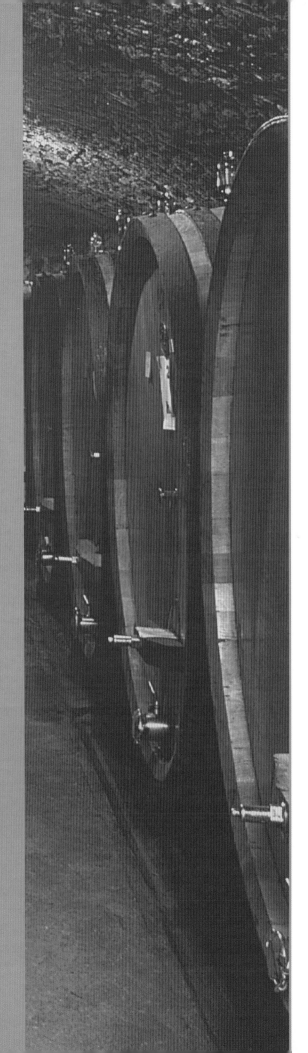

WINEGROWERS
WE HAVE MET

We think we are doing a favour to many wine lovers, by indicating the wine producing firms we encountered during our journey. We do not want to express personal opinions or make a list of these firms. Our intention is to make suggestions for those who want to discover some excellent wines produced on wine farms which have become famous in recent years for the excellent quality of their wines.

SAN CASCIANO IN VAL DI PESA
Antinori
Castelli del Greve Pesa
Conti Serristori
Il Mandorlo
Villa Le Corti

TAVARNELLE VAL DI PESA
Casa Emma

BARBERINO VAL D'ELSA
Quercia al Poggio
Castello di Monsanto

GREVE IN CHIANTI
Carobbio
Castello di Querceto
Castello da Verrazzano
Fontodi
Le Cinciole
Monte Bernardi
Nozzole
Querciabella
Vignamaggio
Villa Calcinaia

CASTELLINA IN CHIANTI
Buondonno

Castello di Fonterutoli
Cecchi
Lilliano
Nittardi
Poggio ai Mori
Rocca delle Macie
Rodano

RADDA IN CHIANTI
Brancaia
Castello d'Albola
Castello di Volpaia
Montevertine
Podere Terreno
Terrabianca
Vignavecchia
Vistarenni

GAIOLE IN CHIANTI
Agricoltori del Chianti Geografico
Badia a Coltibuono
Capannelle
Castello di Brolio
Castello di Cacchiano
Castello di Meleto
Castello di San Polo in Rosso
Il Colombaio di Cencio
Castello di Ama

CASTELNUOVO BERARDENGA
Aiola
Castell'in Villa
Terra Bianca
San Felice

POGGIBONSI
Melini

The Communes of the Chianti Classico

SAN CASCIANO IN VAL DI PESA, TAVARNELLE VAL DI PESA,

BARBERINO VAL D'ELSA, GREVE IN CHIANTI,

CASTELLINA IN CHIANTI, RADDA IN CHIANTI,

GAIOLE IN CHIANTI, CASTELNUOVO BERARDENGA, POGGIBONSI.

*Other notes can be found on the following pages
to complete the material collected during our journey.*

San Casciano in Val di Pesa

Art

Museo della Misericordia Church of Santa Maria al Prato: Simone Martini (attr.), *Crucifix*, painting, 1321-1325; Giovanni di Balduccio, *Annunciation*, marble pulpit, first half of 14th century; Ugolino di Nerio, *Madonna and Child*, first half of 14th century.
Museum of Sacred Art Church of Santa Maria del Gesù: Coppo di Marcovaldo (attr.), *St. Michael the Archangel and the Story of the Legend*, altar frontal, middle of 13th century; Ambrogio Lorenzetti, *Madonna and Child*, painting, 1319; Lippo di Benivieni, *Madonna and Child*, painting, first half of 14th century; Master of Cabestany, *Base of Baptismal Font in Alabaster*, second half of 12th century.

Other sacred and profane buildings

Church of Santa Cecilia a Decimo It is one of the most ancient in the area of San Casciano (10th-11th century) even if the Romanesque elements of the façade have been lost.
Church of Sant'Andrea a Luiano A small, almost intact masterpiece of Chianti Romanesque.
Castello del Pergolato An interesting style of architecture dating back to the 10th century and reminiscent of the architectural features of German castles with "a large circle of walls surrounding a square with a door, with towers and doors on the walls".
The marked 18th century restructuring is clearly visible.

Feasts and events

Le Corti del Vino Villa Le Corti, via San Piero di Sotto 1, end of May-beginning of June. Carefully selected, high quality wines from all over Tuscany.

Mercatino di Ieri (antiques market), Two appointments a year, one in April, the other in June. Location: Cerbaia.

Merc'antico First week in April. Mercatale Val di Pesa.

Handicrafts and shops

Antica Spezieria Piazza Orazio Pierozzi.
Compagnia della Cinta Senese Sales of cured meat and salami, via di Faltignano, 76.

Ceramiche artistiche Ceccarelli Very sophisticated pottery for interior decoration, related to traditions with a few innovative elements. Flower-boxes, fountains, mural panels, garden statues, tables and even delightful sundials, all handmade. Mercatale Val di Pesa.

Restaurants

Il Fedino Traditional Tuscan Chianti cuisine, via Borromeo 9.
Cantinetta Macchiavelli Sant'Andrea in Percussina.

La Tenda Rossa has been, for many years, one of the most interesting restaurants in Tuscany. Here the owner, Silvano Santandrea, with the help of his wife, a refined cook, and his childrẹn, seems to have adopted a philosophy founded on… surprise. The Tenda Rossa is indeed a restaurant where experiments are made and new dishes proposed, a restaurant that continuously renews the menu. "We have to keep our links with our origins" says Santandrea "but the cookery of today and tomorrow will be something different from the traditional one. If we use fine quality ingredients which maintain their unadulterated taste, it is wrong to cover them with sauces and spices. The secret consists in enhancing their natural tastes and this can also be done with the help of modern technology which allows different degrees of cooking and temperatures." Following his advice, we tasted the 'Calf's liver with leek fondue' and the 'Black Raviolini stuffed with lean pork and Tropea onions." Cerbaia.

The architectural structure of the Castle of San Casciano *still shows the crossroads of the road to Rome, formed by the intersection of the Royal Roman Road with the one uniting the Val di Pesa to the Val di Greve, around which grew the borgo in the 13th century. After having been under the dominion of the Florentine bishops in 1272, San Casciano came under the direct control of the Florentine Republic to which it did a great service, protecting it from the fury of its enemies, as in 1326 when the small borough and the surrounding territories were destroyed and overrun by some of the troops of Castruccio Castracani.*
The construction of the walls dates back to the first half of the 14th century. Today it is possible to see only the surviving part which includes one of the two formerly existing doors and the sturdy mastio, the stronghold. Inside the walls can be found the church of Santa Maria al Prato, a building with a nave, built in the 14th century and full of works of art, the 18th century Collegiata of San Cassiano and the church of St. Francis dating back to the middle of the 15th century.

Tavarnelle Val di Pesa

Art

Church of San Biagio a Passignano
Michele di Ridolfo del Ghirlandaio,
Three Saints, Badia a Passignano.

Museum of Sacred Art Church of San
Pietro in Bossolo: Meliore (attr.), *Madonna
with Child and Angels*, painting, 1270-1280;
Ugolino di Nerio (attr.) *Madonna and Child
between St. Peter and St. John the Evangelist*,
triptych, first half of 14th century. His
apprenticeship in the workshop of Duccio
di Buoninsegna can be identified in the
"fine features of the faces, especially that
of the Virgin, the elaborate decorations
still in Gothic style, highlighting the bor-
ders of her blue cloak and the vivid tones
of the colours"; Master of Tavarnelle,
*Madonna enthroned between St. Martin and
St. Sebastian*, altarpiece, beginning of the
16th century; Jacopo Chimenti, known as
l'Empoli, an important master of late
Florentine Mannerism, *Madonna and Child
with St.John*, painting.

Church of San Donato in Poggio
Giovanni della Robbia, *Baptismal Font*,
second half of 15th century,
San Donato in Poggio.

Santuario Madonna di Pietracupa A fine
17th century building, surrounded by a
loggia that served as a shelter for pilgrims.
It is an important example of late
Renaissance architecture, inspired by
Florentine 15th century buildings.

Museum of Peasant Culture San Donato
in Poggio.

Feasts and Events

April Fair In piazza Malaspina, at the end
of the month.

Handicrafts and shops

Bottega d'Arte Even if we are more interested in antique furniture, this shop, using
the techniques of former times, reproduces
high quality period furniture, mostly in
naturally seasoned walnut finish with shel-
lac and beeswax. Via Borghetto 20.

Restaurants

Bottega e Osteria di Passignano During his
childhood, Marcello Crini used to observe
his grandmother and mother busy making
soups, sauces, gravy and roasts, fascinated
by their culinary skills and inebriated by
those familiar aromas. When he grew up,
he wanted to become... a great chef. Then
he got a job in a bank and when he had
reached a certain economic security,
he again had this idea of his strongest
passion: cooking. He opened a delightful
restaurant at Tavarnelle, the Salotto del
Chianti, which he ran with his wife Milva
for several years, earning flattering cri-
ticism in the most renowned magazines and guide-books in the sector. More recently, he was drawn by
the temptation of a new
enterprise and became the
sole proprietor of the
Osteria di Passignano to
which he has dedicated his
sound experience. It con-
sists in a traditional, but
continuously renewed

cuisine and in his extraordinary capacity for discovering new tastes. In the adjacent Bottega, run by Allegra Antinori, one of the daughters of Marchese Piero, you can find a vast choice of wines of the estate. Badia a Passignano.

From Roman times till the Middle Ages, as testified by the 15th century Florentine Property Registry of Tavarnelle Val di Pesa, the small town situated on the road connecting Florence to France, could offer a resting place for those who were passing through as shown by its first name, Taberna, from which its present name is derived. Later, it became a market place for the castles of San Casciano, Tignano and San Donato in Poggio, that is, the market where things were bought and sold. Protected by these castles, Tavarnelle was never fortified and experienced a substantial economic growth only from the first half of the 19th century, the period when permission to hold a weekly market was granted and the Palazzo del Comune, (Municipality) was built.

Barberino Val d'Elsa

Art

Museo Antiquarium Church of Sant'Appiano: many archaeological remains which go from the 8th to the 2nd century BC, are preserved here. They come from several Etruscan 'chamber' tombs, discovered at the beginning of the 20th century near the church. There are articles of Attic pottery with black and red figures (6th–4th century BC), besides some funeral urns in alabaster belonging to the Hellenistic period.

Other sacred and profane buildings

Chapel of San Michele Arcangelo in Semifonte In the vicinity of Petrognano is a small Florentine, late Renaissance jewel. In these parts it is known as the 'Cupolino'. The building was designed by the painter and architect Santi di Tito from 1594-1597. Worthy of note is the small dome, a scale reproduction of the Dome in Florence.

Castello della Paneretta Dating back to the 15th century. It has now been transformed by subsequent restorations but on the whole, it has maintained the solid, crenellated structure of the walls, united by circular towers.

Castello di Tignano Its original structure of a fortified village has remained intact. Inside the walls with a circular plan, there is an imposing square with a 15th century church called Sant'Anna.

Restaurants

Trattoria il Frantoio Marcialla.

Il Paese dei Campanelli A lovely farmhouse divided into four rooms, furnished in good taste reminiscent of the fairy tales of our childhood. This original decoration is reflected in the imaginative arrangement of its skilfully prepared excellent dishes. Petrognano.

The castle of **Barberino Val d'Elsa,**
About which we have no information prior to the 13th century, gained historical importance after the destruction of Semifonte, a small flourishing town razed to the ground by the Florentines in 1202. From then on, the borgo began to expand, thanks also to its suitable position on the territory, situated on the road which connected Florence to France. As it also linked Rome to the countries on the other side of the Alps, it became an important junction for commercial traffic and trade. In the middle of the 13th century, Barberino became the main town of a vast area controlled by Florence, going from the Val d'Elsa to the Val di Pesa. The borgo, surrounded by

the medieval walls, most of which in good condition, has an interesting, elliptic shape preserving many of its original buildings such as Palazzo Barberini and Palazzo Pretorio on whose façade can be seen the coats of arms of noble families.

Greve in Chianti

Art

Museo Comunale di Arte Sacra (Municipal Museum of Sacred Art). It is currently being organized inside the 15th century monastery of St. Francis, situated on a slope at the beginning of the old road leading to Montefioralle, with an annexe containing an archaeological section which will exhibit objects from excavations from areas around the district of Greve. There will also be collections of works by important masters including Nanni di Bartolo and Francesco Granacci who was a leading painter of the Florentine Renaissance and friend and supporter of the young Michelangelo.

Chiesa di Santa Croce Bicci di Lorenzo, *Madonna with Child and Saints,* triptych, middle of 15th century.

Pieve di San Leolino Meliore di Jacopo (attr.), *Madonna enthroned between St. Peter and St.Paul,* altarpiece, middle of 13th century; Taddeo Gaddi, *Madonna with Child and Saints,* triptych, 1421.

Chiesa di Santo Stefano a Montefioralle Master of Montefioralle, *Madonna and Child,* painting, 13th century. Montefioralle.

Other sacred and profane buildings

Oratorio di Sant'Eufrosino Dedicated to the saint and preacher of the Chianti. The building which dates back to the 15th century, has only one nave in the interior with a sloping roof covered by a ribbed vault. Panzano.

Castello di Sezzate Still well preserved, it took on its present aspect in the 14th century when it was built on the ruins of an ancient Roman building. Cintoia.

Castello di Querceto The foundations belong to the Longobard period, even if today the only surviving parts of the medieval castle are the walls and the castle-keep.

Feasts and Events

Open Wine-Cellars It is an event involving all Tuscany and was created to diffuse the culture of quality wines. Every Chianti Commune takes part in this initiative in different periods of the year, opening the doors of the wine-cellars of numerous estates where visitors can taste the different products.

Biannual Exhibition of Contemporary Art in the Chianti It is held on several dates from October to April.

Flower Show Multicoloured, sweet-scented flowers at the beginning of April.

Chianti Classico Wine Show It is the largest wine show in the Chianti, organized with the collaboration of the Consortium of Historical Wines, the fame of which has now spread beyond the boundaries of Tuscany. It takes place during the second week-end in September.

Feast of Peasant Civilization 25th April and 1st May. Strada in Chianti.

Vino al Vino Wine Show Third week-end in September. Panzano.

Handicrafts and Shops

La Bottega dell'artigianato Piazza Matteotti. Unique pieces in wicker and olive wood.

Restaurants

The Wine-Cellars of Greve in Chianti It is an idea which should be further developed. In the old cellars of Greve, the Falorni family has re-designed the look of the already beautiful place with a wine-cellar offering a vast choice of wines not only from Tuscany. They give you the possibility of tasting (almost free of charge) a certain number of wines, having the dual task of encouraging our acquaintance with wine and, consequently, its purchase. But wine should be drunk with something, and this is where the famous cured meat produced by Falorni comes to our aid. Galleria delle Cantine 2.

Enoteca del Chianti Classico It has the severe and reliable appearance of a wine university with the bottles shown in the correct way and an elegant stall where the wines can be tasted by experts. Panzano.

Le Cernacchie This is a gem of Chianti cooking where the owners have presented the dishes for a long time, without giving in to new trends. The atmosphere of the place also contributes to its success. La Panca.

Borgo Antico In this restaurant the food is traditional, even if a bit of imagination

would be advisable. The choice of wines is good. Dimezzano (Lucolena).

Castello di Vicchiomaggio Florentine crèpes' and 'roast-beef with green pepper' seemed to be, among other dishes, two of the finest. Vicchiomaggio.

Trattoria del Montagliari Giovanni Cappelli, the exceptional founder of this restaurant with a typical Chianti atmosphere, has recently sold it to new owners who continue on the same lines as the founder, with enthusiasm and intelligence, introducing a few successful personal touches. Montagliari.

Il Vescovino It is one of the most popular restaurants in the Chianti and, after a period of decline, it is once again able to cope with the demanding palates of its customers. Panzano.

Da Padellina Excellent traditional cuisine. The lively owner knows all the Divine Comedy by heart. Strada in Chianti.

Greve in Chianti

owes its growth from being the small borgo in the Middle Ages, when it was one of the Florentine properties of the Diocese of Fiesole, to its function as a market town, attracting each week a large number of people interested in selling, buying or trading goods of all kinds.

The large square, piazza Matteotti, with its elliptic shape, surrounded by buildings with beautiful terraced loggias which go back to the 16th-17th century, testifies to this ancient vocation.

Situated in a favourable geographic position, the borgo became the centre of trade for the inhabitants of many castles of the surroundings.

The most important of these was Montefioralle which still preserves its original medieval structure. This is also the case of the castle of Panzano dating back to the 12th-13th century, whose two towers and imposing castle keep can still be admired today. In the

18th century, thanks to the growing economic and commercial importance gained, which led to a high increase of the population, it became the main town of the Leopoldine community. Not far from Panzano, a few kilometres from Greve, is the church of San Leolino, whose foundations seem to date back to the 10th century. It is one of the most ancient of the area and stands out for its pure Romanesque forms, visible in the division of the spaces between the two aisles and the nave, marked by arches placed over alabaster pillars.

Castellina in Chianti

Art

Chiesa di San Giorgio Cosimo Rosselli, *Madonna with Child and St.George and St.Francis*, 15th century painting.

Feasts and Events

Pentecost in Castellina in Chianti Friday and Sunday of Pentecost, in the main road of the village.

Restaurants

Trattoria Gallopapa It is hidden in the most ancient part of Castellina.
The restaurant has an atmosphere of a real trattoria with all the elements which distinguish Tuscan catering. Doors open, a visible kitchen, waiters with aprons. Among the most interesting proposals is the delicious meat braised with Vin Santo. Via delle Volte 14/16.
Vintage Wine-Cellar of Palazzo Squarcialupi Owned by Bruno Castelli. Collection of wines and sale of selected Chianti Classico and other wines. Palazzo Squarcialupi. Via Ferruccio 24/26.
Albergaccio di Castellina We recommend 'Lamb stewed with saffron in stimmi' and the tasty 'Polenta timbale with leek purée'. Via Fiorentina 63.

Osteria della **Piazza** It offers a traditional and well prepared menu. The location in an old farmhouse in the main square is particularly congenial.

*T*he findings that testify to the presence *of Etruscan and Roman settlements on the territory of Castellina in Chianti are numerous and significant. The locality is mentioned for the first time as a possession of the Signori del Trebbio. Their castle came under the dominion of Florence in 1193. After the foundation of the Chianti League, Castellina became the main town of one of the three parts and following the Lodo of Poggibonsi, 1203, it became an important fortified stronghold of the Florentines on the road connecting Siena to Florence. Owing to its geographical position, the borgo became subject in 1397 to looting and destruction by the Sienese armies, allied to the Duke of Milan under the leadership of Alberico da Barbiano. The building of new fortifications put an end to this devastation but had to be strengthened 30 years later, following the plans by Brunelleschi, sent to Castellina by the Opera del Duomo to examine the conditions. After having resisted the attack of the Aragonese army in the middle of the 15th century, the fortifications surrendered to the attack of Sienese troops in 1478. This time, Siena was supported by the powerful militia of Naples. We can still appreciate the underground passageway of the ancient walls in the southern part of the circle of walls and the powerful stronghold, now the headquarters of the Municipality.*

Radda in Chianti

Art

Museum of Sacred Art of the Chianti This museum which is still being organized in the former Franciscan monastery of Santa Maria in Prato, will contain most of the artistic heritage of the Sienese Chianti. Among the most important works, should be mentioned the *Madonna dei Raccomandati* by Simone Martini and Memo di Filippuccio, the *Polittici* by Bernardo Daddi and Luca di Tommè da Venano and a fine triptych by Bicci di Lorenzo.

Church of Santa Maria in Prato It dates back to the 11th century and to the site of a small Franciscan monastery, *Madonna and Child among Saints Nicola of Bari, St.John the Baptist, Mary Magdalene and St.Anthony Abate,* painting, 1474.

Feasts and Events

Vacanza Antiquaria Fine quality furniture and simple handicrafts, ornaments and furniture between the old and the new, at Easter and in September.
Antiques and Junk Fair Good Friday and Easter Monday.
Open Wine-Cellars Several wine producers of the area open their cellars to the public where they can taste the wines of the year. From the end of May to the beginning of June.

Handicrafts and Shops

The Ice-box of the Grand Duchy In the times of the Grand Duchy of Tuscany, were built wall structures in numerous areas to preserve snow which, when pressed, would be transformed into cold blocks of ice where they could preserve food for long periods. To enable this process, it was important for these constructions to be oriented towards the north, for the walls to have a sufficient thickness to guarantee a constantly low temperature and for the ice-box to be built like a pyramid or in the shape of a cone, as in the case of Radda in Chianti.

It is in this very same imposing building that a fascinating shop has been opened, lit with warm floodlighting and a floor of wooden planks. It is a unique shop where lovers of antiques and fine quality handicrafts can enjoy browsing among the numerous beautiful objects shown and, perhaps, end up by buying something. Rampini Ceramics is an institution of ceramics in the Chianti. Romano Rampini, a well-known maestro, produces handmade pottery and articles in Tuscan and Umbrian tradition, especially striking jugs, plates and dinnersets, all hand-painted.

We particularly fell in love particularly with a large jug for infusions, decorated with Renaissance emblems, showing a personal touch of the maestro. Casa Beretone di Vistarenni.

"Casa Porciatti"

The awarded firm Porciatti is a speciality of the Chianti region, and particularly of the Siena area. This butcher's shop offers uniquely prepared pork and a variety of exquisite delicatessen products. Near by you can find an equally extraordinary wine shop.

Restaurants

Relais Vignale Enoteca, restaurant, wine-cellar. A first rate relais in the very heart of Radda, an enoteca of selected wines, a qualified restaurant with typical Chianti style dishes, renewed by an imaginative spirit.

La Cantoniera di Vescine Excellent atmosphere, hospitality and services. We ate a good filet of beef in Marsala sauce and patée de foie gras. Vescine.

Cavini Cured meat, cheese and a good glass of wine. Lucarelli.

An ancient document *drawn up in 1002, signed by Emperor Otto III, mentions for the first time the existence of the castle of Radda and its donation by Countess Willa to Badia Fiorentina. In 1191 Radda came under the dominion of the Conti Guidi. When it came under Florentine domination in the 13th century, it underwent destruction and looting by the Sienese (1230), the troops of Charles d'Anjou (1268) and by the Aragonese in the second half of the 15th century. Meanwhile, at the beginning of the 14th century Florence had founded the Lega del Chianti that divided the entire territory into three equal parts choosing Radda as the main town of one of them and later, in 1415, of the entire League. Due to the continuous attacks of the Sienese, the borgo had been surrounded by a circle of walls as far back as 1300. But the work had to be resumed two centuries later, owing to the severe damage caused by the Aragonese troops. Unfortunately, only parts of the walls and a few towers have survived, whilst the gates have disappeared altogether. In the small borgo, Palazzo del Podestà is a 15th century construction whose façade, decorated with coats of arms, opens onto a small loggia. In front of it is the rectory of San Niccolò f medieval origin which has lost its Romanesque characteristics, owing to modern restructuring.*

Gaiole in Chianti

Sacred and profane buildings
Church of Santa Maria a Spaltenna The fortified religious complex of Spartenna, has preserved its Romanesque structures. The wall outside is covered with Albarese, whereas the apse presents original, large Gothic windows.

Church of San Vincenti One of the most ancient in the Chianti (it had already been mentioned in the 7th century). It appears today as a construction of the 13th-14th century with a semicircular apse and an interior with a nave and two aisles, divided by round arches supported by pillars.

Castello di Vertine Was a fortress before 1000 and the site of a *curtis* and thus it played an important role in the territory. It now has the characteristics of a fortified borgo, one of the finest of the Chianti area. It is surrounded by a circle of walls, still partly intact, and by several towers and a noble palace, covered with alberese. The entrance door is very beautiful. Above it, is a round arch showing stylistically Sienese elements.

Torre di Barbischio The tower at the top of the borgo is an exceptional example of a combination of ancient and modern architecture. It was rebuilt a few years ago by a Florentine businessman, Franco Innocenti, who fell in love with the few surviving ruins and decided to live there and become a painter.

There are also the castles of Lucignano, Tornano, Lecchi and Castagnoli, all fascinating fortifications only a few kilometres away.

Feasts and Events
September in Gaiole The first week-end of the month, in the Piazza del Comune.

Wine festival and Tournament of the Rioni Second Sunday in September.

Restaurants

Wilhelm's Chianti
The other side of the volume we stopped for a moment to look at the more esteemed of the new vineyards in the

Chianti, the Colombaio di Cencio. But Werner Wilhelm didn't stop at this. In the environs of Gaiole he has restored some fantastic farmhouses into an exclusive farmhouse hotel with swimming pool and a style which adheres perfectly to the local taste. In the locality of Vinci, between Gaiole and the beautiful tower at Barbischio, there is a restaurant which by now has a consolidated fame. It is called Le Contrade. Managed by daughter Stefania, a name which was in honour of the passion which the German entrepreneur holds for Siena and the Palio horse race. It is a restaurant with a finesse which is put forward in a double guise. It has been arranged that lunch will be enjoyed on the beautiful terrace which looks onto the Chianti. This is the time for light and refreshing dishes. At dinner the atmosphere and menu change. We are hosted inside the building with an elegant atmosphere and we are brought fine Tuscan dishes. All of which is naturally washed down with wines from the Colombaio di Cencio.

Castello di Spaltenna An ancient, fortified monastery where it is possible to dine under the Chianti sky in summer, in an elegant atmosphere. We are agreeably surprised by the 'Risotto with asparagus tips' and the warm 'Wild endive salad seasoned with balsamic vinegar'. Via Spaltenna 13.

Trattoria Badia a Coltibuono
We came here with the intention of tasting their excellent, traditional dishes but what is really traditional are the ingredients used for the Tuscan recipes prepared by a skilful, cultured and creative chef. Coltibuono.

Osteria del Castello di Brolio Brolio.

La Grotta Hotel. That which was once a small fortress in the IX century and a stopping place to rest before going onwards to the nearby church of Brolio, is today a hotel with an unconventional elegance. The atmosphere is similar to that found in a noble and welcoming house whose owners share with you the pleasure of living in the beauty that surrounds the house. An interesting kitchen welcomes the "modern" traveller who will be able to refresh himself by taking a dip in one of the two swimming pools which is almost unique in the Chianti.

Trattoria il Papavero In this small, charming restaurant, Yvonne and Franco Innocenti welcome their customers and a few faithful friends, proposing their dishes prepared by a skilful cook and accompanied by good wines. Barbischio.

Gaiole in Chianti *situated at the foot of the pass that goes to the Val d'Arno through the hills of the Chianti, it became a vital, flourishing borgo in the 13th century. After the* curterese *economic crisis and that of the neighbouring castles of Barbischio and Vertine, for many years the centre of commerce and trade, it shifted the activity of the area which became the market centre and, subsequently the main town of one of the three parts of the League of the Chianti. The village is crossed by a road which goes through the area and widens, becoming an elongated, triangular square. Numerous shops were opened and still face the square, revealing its medieval origin, even if the buildings on either side are modern and very* *few architectural elements belong to the past. In the 18th century, Grand Duke Leopold spoke of Gaiole as a busy trading and commercial centre and the site of an important fair, held every year in the month of December.*

Castelnuovo Berardenga

Art

Certosa di Pontignano Founded in 1343, the 16th century cloister, onto which the 14th century façade of the original church opens, is very interesting. Inside, the frescos on the vaults are by Bernardino Poccetti and assistants. He was a Florentine master of the late 16th century who also painted the beautiful *Last Supper* in the refectory. A small museum is being organized where the works from several rooms of the large complex will be placed, including two 14th century wooden *Crucifixes*.

Church of San Cristoforo a Vagliagli *Baptismal Font.*

Museum of the Chianti Landscape.

Other sacred and profane buildings

Pieve of Pievasciata One of the numerous Romanesque churches in the Chianti. The fortified structure has a very beautiful belltower in alberese which looks like a castle keep.

Monastero di San Salvatore o Badia Monastero Dating back to 867. This very ancient abbey, commissioned by the noblemen of La Berardenga has now been transformed into a rural villa whose structures develop around the original cloisters. The sturdy, square belltower is not only fascinating but undoubtedly the finest example of Lombard Romanesque architecture in the Chianti. This style is evident in the rhythmic alternation of two tiers of single mullioned and three tiers of three mullioned windows.

Castello di Fagnano Grandiose and refined structure commissioned by Giovan Battista Piccolomini in the style of a fortified villa with a large Italian garden. Like other buildings and structures of the kind, the castle has been entirely restructured in neo-Gothic style.

Castell'in Villa The large, high medieval stone tower and the adjacent church offer a striking spectacle. They are part of a more ancient, fascinating fortification, dating back to the Conti della Berardenga, who lived in the Chianti before 1000.

Castello-borgo di San Gusmé Already mentioned in 867, San Gusmé is an inhabited borgo with one of the most important Sienese strongholds. Large parts of the original layout still exist, including the original doors, the stone streets and a theatrical atmosphere in the costumes of those times.

Feasts and Events

The Feast of Good Friday Procession in costume to commemorate the 'Stations of the Cross'.

The Banner of the Rioni and the Comuni Historical commemoration held in June at the stadium or in the historical centre of the town with the 'donkey race'.

The Banner of the donkeys Takes place in the first week of September.

Commemoration of the Battle of Monteaperti Where the Florentines and the Sienese challenged each other in battle in 1260.

Feast of the Grape Organized at the end of September, Vagliagli.

Handicrafts and Shops

Quinquatrus, la Bottega delle Arti This is a really special shop showing articles of a high level of craftsmanship, among which decorated ceramic table-sets, blown glass, articles in wrought iron, wooden objects, fine embroidered table-cloths, all in good taste and strictly handmade. But for those who are real lovers of handmade things, interesting courses are organized in the area every month. Courses are also held for those who want to learn the art of weaving, painting on ceramics, furniture restoration or the creation of original decorations for Christmas but also for the other months of the year.

Restaurants

La Bottega del Trenta The beautiful farmhouse which dates back to the middle ages is agreeably furnished. We ate a large aubergine 'timbale' with tomato sauce and a rabbit marinated with vinegar and apples, worthy of the best of Vissani. Villa a Sesta.

The '**Terra Berardinga**', *already mentioned in ancient documents which date back to the 11th century, includes that vast territory between the Ombrone and the Arbia, the Chianti and the Crete which was occupied by the ancient family of the Uburgeri della Berardenga from which it takes its name. In 1366, the Great Council of the Sienese Republic officially decreed the existence of the castle, then called Castelnuovo, to distinguish it from the more ancient castles of Arceno and Valcortese. The borgo was defended by the fortifications which were destroyed by the army of Giovanni Acuto, called by the English John Hawkwood, a captain of good fortune in the services of Florence. The alternate vicissitudes of Florence and Siena ended in the defeat of the latter and the annexation in 1555 of Castelnuovo Berardenga by the Grand Duchy of Tuscany.*

More Notes About Art

For art lovers, we want to mention some masterpieces just outside the boundaries of the Chianti Classico.

Collegiata di Santa Maria dell'Impruneta Museo del Tesoro, one of the most important collections of silver, illuminated codices and Florentine religious vestments (1400-1800). Impruneta.

Monastery of San Lucchese It is a rare example of a mixture of Romanesque and Gothic. The ancient Franciscan monastery is a small museum containing important works. Gerino da Pistoia, *Multiplication of the loaves and the fish.* Frescos, 1513, Poggibonsi.

Church of Santa Maria Assunta Collection of Sacred Art Antonio del Pollaiolo, *Mary Magdalen announced by angels*, painting, 6th decade of the 15th century; Francesco Botticini, *Adoration of the Magi, painting,* second half of the 15 th century, Staggia Senese, tavola, sesto decennio del '400; Francesco Botticini, *Adorazione dei Magi.*

Badia dei Santi Salvatore e Cirino Known as **Badia a Isola** It is one of the most beautiful romanesque bulildings in Val d'Elsa. It was certainly taken as an example for the building of many Romanesque Churches in the Chianti. Sano di Pietro *Madonna with Child and Saints*, painting, first half of 15th century, Moteriggioni.

BIBLIOGRAPHY

AA. VV., *Il Chianti e la Valdelsa Senese*, Firenze 2000.

AA. VV., *Dal kantharos alla bordolese*, Centro di studi chiantigiani "Clante", Poggibonsi 2000.

AA. VV., *Civiltà romanica nel Chianti*, Centro di studi chiantigiani "Clante", Poggibonsi 1995.

AA. VV., *Il Monachesimo medievale in Chianti*, Centro di studi chiantigiani "Clante", Poggibonsi 1995.

AA. VV., *"Imago Clantis"*, Centro di studi chiantigiani "Clante", Poggibonsi 1993.

AA. VV., *Il Paesaggio Riconosciuto. Luoghi, Architetture e opere d'arte nella provincia di Firenze*, Milano 1984.

AA. VV., *Il Chianti*, Centro di studi storici chiantigiani, Firenze 1984.

R. Barbaresi, D. Di Bello, *Il Chianti di San Felice*, Tavarnelle Val di Pesa 2000.

E. Bosi, G. L. Scarfiotti, *Di castello in castello. Il Chianti*, Firenze 1990.

M. Bossi, M. Seidel (a cura di), *Viaggio in Toscana*, Venezia 1998.

G. Branchetti Montorselli, I. Moretti, R. Stopani, *Le strade del Chianti Gallo Nero*, Firenze 1984.

F. Cardini, *Il Medioevo in Toscana*, Firenze 1992.

A. Casabianca, *Notizie storiche sui principali luoghi del Chianti*, Firenze 1941.

R. P. Ciardi, A. Natali (a cura di), *Il Cinquecento. Storia delle arti in Toscana*, Firenze 2000.

M. Frati, *Chiese romaniche della campagna fiorentina*, Pisa 1997.

S. Manetti, *Vino e Cucina. Divagazioni erogastronomiche*, Firenze 1995.

E. Massei, *Artigianato del Chianti. Radici, modelli e tradizioni*, Firenze 2000.

I. Moretti, *Case da signore e case da lavoratore*, Pistoia 1986.

I. Moretti, R. Stopani, *Chiese romaniche nel Chianti*, Firenze 1996.

I. Moretti, R. Stopani, *I castelli dell'antica Lega del Chianti*, Firenze 1972.

A. Polvani, G. Merlini, L. De Filla, T. Polvani, I. Pianigiani, C. Peroni , *Il Chianti di Montefienali*, Firenze 2004

R. C. Proto Pisani, *Il Museo di Arte Sacra a San Casciano Val di Pesa*, Siena 1992.

E. Repetti, *Dizionario geografico fisico storico del Granducato di Toscana*, Firenze 1972.

L. Rombai, R. Stopani, *Il Chianti*, Milano 1981.

M. C. Salemi, Chianti. *Leggenda, storia e qualità del principe della tavola, simbolo di un territorio*, Firenze 1999.

R. Stopani, *Un Santuario Altomedievale nel Chianti*, Centro di studi chiantigiani "Clante", Poggibonsi 1998.

Printed in Italy in August 2004

Arte Tipolitografica Italiana Spa - Pomezia (Rome)
atispa@atispa.com